G000038370

Intellectual Capital

Navigating the New Business Landscape

Johan Roos, Göran Roos,
Nicola Carlo Dragonetti
and Leif Edvinsson

MACMILLAN
Business

First published 1997 by
MACMILLAN PRESS LTD
Houndmills, Basingstoke, Hampshire RG21 6XS
and London
Companies and representatives throughout the world

ISBN 0–333–69479–1

A catalogue record for this book is available
from the British Library.

This book is printed on paper suitable for recycling and
made from fully managed and sustained forest sources.

10   9   8   7   6   5   4
06   05   04   03   02   01   00   99   98

Editing and origination by
Aardvark Editorial, Mendham, Suffolk

Printed in Great Britain by
Creative Print and Design (Wales), Ebbw Vale

Contents

Executive Summary

This book discusses and illustrates in a practical way the first steps managers must take to develop an intellectual capital approach in their own companies (Chapters 2–3). Moreover, it introduces new and unique techniques developed by the authors, in particular the intellectual capital index approach (Chapter 4) and how to connect intellectual capital to shareholder value creation (Chapter 5).

Throughout this book it will be evident that we see *intellectual capital as a language for thinking, talking and doing something about the drivers of companies' future earnings*. Intellectual capital comprises relationships with customers and partners, innovation efforts, company infrastructure and the knowledge and skills of organizational members. As a concept, intellectual capital comes with a set of techniques that enable managers to manage better.

Although intellectual capital is the starting point for all businesses, during the past ten years it has considerably increased its role in the value creation process. This is due to fundamental changes in society and the business world. A quick examination of the nature of the most valuable companies today, for instance, provides a clear message. Services and solutions have slowly but surely replaced the single-product sale mentality of the industrial era: knowledge and information are now the most important resources a company can muster.

The increasing importance of knowledge for the sustainability of companies has encouraged the development of many new, or at least modified, management theories. Two streams of contributions can be highlighted. On one side, authors have prescribed different ways to generate, increase and exploit knowledge. On the other side, much attention has focused on the problem of measuring knowledge. The concept of intellectual capital represents the fusion between these two streams of thoughts: it is concerned with both managing and measuring knowledge and other intangibles in the company. The perspective taken in this book is that these two concerns are two sides of the same coin: what you can measure, you can manage, and what you want to manage, you have to measure.

To manage and measure intellectual capital, it is essential that the *nature* of intellectual capital itself is clear. This is why it is important to distinguish between different forms of intellectual capital, as well as the dynamics among them. Whereas many companies have so far only applied a 'balance sheet' approach to intellectual capital, a complementary 'profit and loss' approach is a natural extension. Thus, flows among the different forms of capital, intellectual and physical, should be measured and managed as much as the stocks. It is these flows that generate and alter the stocks, and it would thus be meaningless to manage one without the other.

A comprehensive system of capturing and measuring intellectual capital must be deeply rooted in the strategy or the mission of the company. Strategy has to guide the search for the appropriate indicators simply because it is the goals and direction of the company, set out in the strategy, that signify which intellectual capital forms are important. If a company states that its goal is to become the most caring service provider in the market, the attention of the company will be on customer relations, relatively more so than on the development of new patents.

So far so good, but for the company that wants to reap more of the benefits of an intellectual capital perspective it is not enough. For instance, at this stage, there is no means of judging what intellectual capital forms or flows are more important than others. Nor can you make meaningful comparisons across units or companies, simply because the intellectual capital system is organization-specific (remember that the strategy was the starting point!). This is why we move into discussing the 'second generation' of intellectual capital practice. In essence this means consolidating intellectual capital measures into one single measure, an IC-Index.

Most management teams have no problem in coming up with a long list of intellectual capital indicators but sometimes it is based more on hunches of what makes sense than on well-grounded theory. Before an IC-Index can be developed, however, it is often necessary to refine the list of indicators and select from it the important few indicators of intellectual capital which can form a robust index that captures what it is intended to capture. As well as providing useful insight into the value-creating dynamics of companies, such an IC-Index has recently also been applied on a industry basis in both Northern Europe and Australia. Recent economic theory about innovation and growth in society provides a solid foundation for connecting changes in companies' intellectual capital (the IC-Index) to changes in both financial performance and, interestingly, shareholder value creation and destruction. In the last part of the book we discuss and illustrate how companies can benefit from this approach, and even improve their ability to predict and influence shareholder value.

Intellectual capital, both as a language and a set of techniques for addressing future earnings capabilities, implies a different meaning of management than the one we are used to. Adopting an intellectual capital perspective in the company means more than supplementing the financial reporting with an intellectual capital report. We end the book with a short elaboration and some illustrations on what it means for management.

The New
Business World

With an incredible US$168 billion in sales General Motors, a company representing the prosperous industrial era, again hit the top spot of the famous *Fortune 500* ranking in 1996. From the perspective of the classical 'factors of production' – land, labour, money, and equipment – the US$222 billion of assets[1] of GM makes it a very wealthy and indeed influential company.

Like GM, many of today's best companies have done their utmost to squeeze every penny out of their hard assets, physical and monetary. Cycle time has been reduced to the bare minimum, inventory is virtually zero, investments are carefully selected in terms of a balance between short-term and long-term resources. On the competitive side, multi-million dollar ad campaigns are launched to conquer every last bit of the potential market, or to scrub away half a percentage point of market share from competitors.

But things are not always what they seem to be in the business world of today. Let's switch around from a sales and hard asset perspective to one that instead places value creation at the forefront. From the sales and asset perspective the performance of the computer software giant Microsoft is not very impressive. Its mere US$9 billion in sales and US$10 billion in assets give it the 172nd place on the *Fortune 500* list of 1996. Though it had only some 5 per cent of the sales and assets of its industrial counterpart GM, the *market value*[2] of Microsoft was US$120 billion in early 1997 and this made it the third most valuable company in the US. Microsoft had nearly $2\frac{1}{2}$ times more market value than the US$50 billion worth of GM. Some raw data of the top five US companies ranked by market value are shown in Table 1.1.[3] The data clearly show that the market value of these companies is many times their net asset value, that is the value of their physical capital. The difference between the two

1

values is the company's 'hidden value', which can be expressed as a percentage of the market value.

Table 1.1   Market value and assets (in billions of dollars)

Company	Market Value	Revenue	Profits	Net Assets	'Hidden Value'
General Electric	169	79	7.3	31	138 (82%)
Coca-Cola	148	19	3.5	6	142 (96%)
Exxon	125	119	7.5	43	82 (66%)
Microsoft	119	9	2.2	7	112 (94%)
Intel	113	21	5.2	17	96 (85%)

Net assets, however, might not be the best way to evaluate a company's physical capital. Different national accounting practices in fact tend to suggest different ways of valuing and depreciating assets, thus distorting the picture. Also, even among companies operating in the same country, there are usually more acceptable methods of evaluation, each leading to a slightly different result: the choice by managers of one method versus the others can once again distort the comparison. All this does not even take into account the 'rule bending' which some companies may apply to present a picture of their situation appropriate to their goals.

These considerations suggest the adoption of a measure of company value which is 'accounting neutral', namely the replacement value of its physical assets. The price the company would have to pay to replace its assets surely does not depend on the particular accounting protocol used. Moreover, it uses data which are most often readily available to a well-managed company.[4]

Although there is no study of the relationship between a company's net assets and the cost of replacing them, let's be generous and assume that the replacement costs are $2\frac{1}{2}$ times the value of net assets. If we deduct this new figure from the market value, the picture changes dramatically, as shown in Table 1.2. The hidden value of some of the companies has now shrunk considerably. Still, a considerable portion of the value of Microsoft, Coca-Cola and Intel is unexplained and unaccounted for.

No matter how this kind of performance is examined the conclusion is obvious. Companies like Intel, Merck, GTE, Microsoft, Wal-Mart and Walt Disney, all with considerably less sales and assets, are far more valuable than many of the industrial giants. Moreover, judged by a performance criterion close to the heart of many CEOs even today, namely return on assets, the difference is considerable. This does not only concern high-tech, consumer-products companies. Take a closer look at Caterpillar, an industrial company with few direct business contacts with the end-users of its earth-moving machinery. The difference between its 1996 net assets of some US$4 billion and the early 1997 market value of some US$15 billion is a lot of money.

Table 1.2 Market value and hypothetical replacement costs (in billions of dollars)

Company	Market Value	Net Assets	Hypothetical Replacement Costs	'Hidden Value'
General Electric	169	31	77	92 (54%)
Coca-Cola	148	6	15	133 (90%)
Exxon	125	43	107	18 (14%)
Microsoft	119	7	18	101 (85%)
Intel	113	17	43	70 (62%)

But what does the huge difference between value of net assets and market value of some companies comprise? In the case of Microsoft it is a breathtaking US$100 billion plus. How much of this value stems from the brands, customer relationships, anticipated new products, or the productivity and motivation of employees? Although this is hard to determine with conventional valuation approaches, it is clear that knowledge, brands, innovation projects, and other 'invisible' assets enable more wealth creation than the classical production factors, and often achieve it much more quickly (we will examine this in Chapter 5).

This is of course why it is not uncommon for a company to be valued at many times its asset value. At the end of the first day of trading, the market valued Netscape at US$3 billion. Its book value? US$17 million, which gives us a nice market-to-book ratio of 176.4. Netscape is an exception, of course. All the same, a quick examination of the companies quoted on Wall Street reveals that the average market-to-book value ratio is close to three. This means that, while the company's assets are valued 100, the total value according to the market is 300. If we examine the most recent acquisitions, the only common factor is that the price paid for the acquired company is almost invariably higher than its book value. This is considered normal, and the difference between the price paid and the book value has been incorporated into accounting practices under the name of goodwill. What has changed recently, and made the phenomenon abnormal, is the size of the goodwill that has been paid.

As far back as 1969 the famous economist John Kenneth Galbraith gave us a hint on how to address this value gap when he coined the concept of 'intellectual capital'. He suggested that intellectual capital means *intellectual action* more than just knowledge or pure intellect. Thus, intellectual capital can be seen *both* as a form of value creation *and* as an asset in its traditional sense. The reason for valuing Caterpillar at almost four times the value of its hard assets derives from all of the 'invisible' value, and *potential for new value creation* stemming from its well-known Cat brand, its unique dealership network recently praised by Don Fites, the CEO of Caterpillar, and the knowledge of its employees. This is also the explanation, of course, for some of the differences shown in Table 1.1.

Clearly, good management has become much more than management of hard assets and 'human resources'. The ability to visualise, measure and report growth or decline in the company's intellectual capital will become an increasingly important managerial capability. Given the high stakes, it seems only fair that the road to a correct understanding of the invisible side of the company is hard and largely unexplored. Some milestones have been set, though, and in this chapter we will examine the evolution of the attempts to chart this no-man's land.

During the 1980s managers realised they were neglecting an important part of their companies, just because it did not show in the financial reporting. Therefore, first we will examine what in the past decade encouraged the development of a theory on invisible assets. Second, we will turn to a description of the evolution of both the management and the measurement schools of thought. We will conclude the chapter with a reflection on the differences between the existing theories in the two schools of thought and the latest development in the field: intellectual capital (IC).

Preparing for the Journey

The evidence we have recounted above lead us to draw a hard conclusion: the world has changed, and dramatically at that. We could be even more drastic: in the modern business world, the business imperative is to manage intellectual capital or die!

This is the main message that we want to convey with this book, but we do not expect you to accept it straightaway. Instead, that statement is going to be the red thread of the whole book, and we will show you, by the time we reach the final chapter, what we mean by 'managing' IC.

The problem is that intellectual capital is a very new and unknown topic. Research into it started just five years ago (even though there has been some previous research in adjacent areas). As a consequence, a book on intellectual capital is like a journey into uncharted territory, where only reason and some good navigation tools can help us to find the way. Our role as authors is going to be to guide you in this journey, providing you with our interpretation of events, reality and theory, and providing you with the tools to create your own IC management system. Unlike other books on intellectual capital, we will not give you a ready-made system which you can just read about and plug into your company. We would rather give you the right tools and the comprehension to tailor-make the intellectual capital system that best suits the need of your particular company. In this sense, we will use a cookbook approach rather than the ready-made one used in some other books.

Our approach will require much more effort on your part than the ready-made one. You will have to understand the theoretical grounding of intellectual capital, and bear through a list of intellectual capital categories and flows. The rewards, however, will be great. As we will show you, an intellectual capital system is good only inasmuch as it supports the company's strategy and/or goals. Thus, we believe it is useless to suggest one particular intellectual capital system over any other, because only the company's managers can make that decision. Our aim instead is to supply you with the appropriate concepts, models and techniques to enable you to develop your own IC approach.

Let's go back to the main purpose we stated before: in the modern business world, the business imperative is to manage intellectual capital or die. Following this statement, our journey in the lands of intellectual capital will be structured in two different 'legs', divided into five chapters (Figure 1.1).

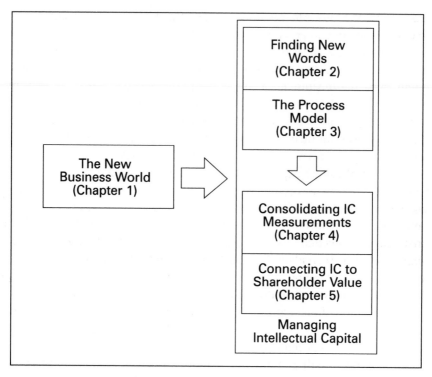

Figure 1.1   The map of the book

The remainder of this first chapter will complete the first leg of the journey, drawing the picture of the new business world. The changes in the economy in the past ten years have made knowledge and information the most important sources of competitive advantage and success a company can have. The challenge, though, is understanding the different dynamics of these two factors, and, indeed, the different economic laws governing them. While land, capital and labour all follow the law of decreasing returns, knowledge and information enjoy increasing returns instead.[6] The consequences of this are staggering. *Any* small victory in the competitive battlefield can now cause unpredictable avalanches of change in the competitive landscape, as it did in the case of Microsoft and its Windows software, or in the case of the VHS standard. This can be good or bad, of course, depending on whether the company is on the winning or losing side. All the same, it surely makes the concept, logic and management of these factors that much more important to understand.

Management theory has not sat idly, witnessing this change in the rules of the game. A veritable multitude of theories has emerged, each trying to capture the essence of the problem – on one side the measurement of the hidden value of the company, and on the other side the management of knowledge and information, as sources of sustainable competitive advantage. No theory, though, until the beginning of the 1990s and the development of the concept of intellectual capital, has realised that the two problems are only two sides of the same coin: what you can measure, you can manage, and what you want to manage, you have to measure. Intellectual capital theory represents the fusion between these two streams of thoughts. IC is concerned with how better to manage and measure knowledge and other intangibles in the company.

Having made the case that knowledge and information have to be managed, and that intellectual capital is the most appropriate theoretical lens to use, the second leg of the journey will examine the task of managing intellectual capital. To this end, it is essential to understand the *nature* of intellectual capital and its different forms, as well as the dynamics among them (see Chapter 2). Whereas many companies have so far applied only a 'balance sheet' approach to IC, a complementary 'profit and loss' approach, also considering the dynamic flows, is a natural extension. Thus, flows among the different forms of capital, intellectual and material, should be analysed and managed as much as the stocks. It is these flows that generate and alter the stocks, and it would thus be meaningless to manage one without the other.

Chapter 3 is essentially a step-by-step guide to the creation of a comprehensive system to capture and measure intellectual capital. Such a system must be deeply rooted in the strategy of the company: strategy has to guide the search for the appropriate indicators simply because it is the goals and direction of the company, set out in the strategy, that signify which intellectual capital forms are important. If a company states that its goal is to become the most caring service provider in the market, the attention of the company will be on customer relations, relatively more so than on the development of new patents. Throughout the chapter, the efforts of three real companies are followed, as an example of what the creation of an IC system implies.

This is as far as all contributions and applications of intellectual capital have gone up to now. While the benefits are evident, so are the limitations. IC systems have long lists of indicators with no prioritisation, thus making it impossible for managers to evaluate trade-off decisions. Moreover, intellectual capital indicators have no relation whatosever to the physical and financial side of companies: in reality, the relationships are all too obvious, and indeed they are the prime reason why intellectual capital should be considered at all. To solve all these problems, the concept of a 'second generation' of intellectual capital practices is introduced.

The first step in a second generation practice is to aggregate the different IC indicators into an IC-Index: Chapter 4 will consider this issue. Consolidation involves first of all a review and refinement of the indicators, to ensure that they are precise and robust enough. Then, weights should be given to each indicator. Not all indicators of intellectual capital will be equally important: some will be more relevant to the company strategy, and some less so. It is then only a matter of carrying out some simple mathematical calculations to create IC indices, at different levels of aggregation, that will help managers guide their companies. The IC-indices will represent a kind of final 'IC bottom line' to test the proposed strategies against.

Although perhaps not representative of the absolute level of stock of intellectual capital, the IC-indices capture changes in this level very well. Knowing these changes, it is only a short step to relate them to the market value of the company, thus understanding the premium the market awards to an IC increase. From there to a full management of shareholder and market value through IC, as well as through financial and physical capital, the journey is short indeed, as Chapter 5 will show. We will conclude the journey with some reflections on the consequences of intellectual capital on management by elaborating on the concept of 'navigation'.

For the interested reader we offer additional references and an expanded discussion of selected concepts and ideas in a series of notes at the end of the book.

The Engine of the New Economy

We are all familiar with the mantra of 'the economy is changing very fast', 'we are witnessing the biggest wave of changes since the Industrial Revolution' and similar refrains. While there is certainly a tendency to overestimate the changes and their magnitude compared to previous 'revolutions', there is no doubt that the economy of 1997 can hardly be compared to the economy of 1897, or that of 1947, for that matter. The changes are not just quantitative but also qualitative.

We are not talking about technological advances here, although these certainly had something to do with it. We want instead to highlight the fact that, today, the prime commodities are knowledge and information, either as the main object of transactions or as a very important component of them.

The impact of what some have already dubbed the 'knowledge economy' is not limited exclusively to the new industries, or to the knowledge-based ones. Think about the epitome of a consumer, mass-produced, standardised product: soap. Pick up a bar of soap from any supermarket. You will notice that packaging fulfills two important roles. The first and more obvious one is the creation of marketing appeal: in a competitive situation where the typical supermarket stocks in excess of 10 000 products, the ability to grab the consumer's attention is essential. The second role, however, is no less important: packaging conveys information. Contents, ingredients, instructions for use, side-effects, promotions and anything else can be featured on the package. Quite a change if you consider that a 100 years ago soap was sold by weight in chemists.

The question, though, still remains: why? Why suddenly this increase in the amount of knowledge and information circulating in the business world? We can identify at least three reasons.

First, and probably most importantly, technological progress have revolutionised the way information is processed and stored. Computers have enabled data processing at low costs and high speed, and made it possible for managers to use more information in their routines. Of course, the ability to use more information suddenly generated a request for more information. This partly explains why consultant services and information research companies experienced such a boom in the 1980s. Improved communication technology, moreover, has increased massively the amount of information circulating in the world, as well as the speed of communication. When Canary Wharf was bombed by the IRA in February 1996, full news report were relayed to the world in less than an hour.

Second, communication technology, together with improved transportation, also created a much closer connection among geographically separate countries and regions. The closer connection in turn increased the complexity of any action, because factors influencing the action could come now from all over the world. For example, the full effects on the economy of the 1929 New York stock market crash were delayed by about three days, until the news reached all the corners of the world; in 1987, however, when Wall Street crashed again, the effects were immediately felt by stock exchanges all over the world. The final effect of these tight links between all the world economies is that more information is needed to act, but one action also generates more information than before.

Third, the level of sophistication of both consumers and strategists has increased. For consumers, this means that they want more for their money (and this 'more' in most cases translates into additional services, that is, information and knowledge) and they want to know more about what they buy. Also, the increased experience of consumers with the products can help the same consumers to understand their needs better, and pinpoint their preferences to companies. The mirror side of this phenomenon is that more sophisticated strategies are required to reach consumers, which, once again, require more information to prepare and implement.

The final result of all these factors is a noticeable shift of the economy from the industry to the service, and even in the industry a shift of the competitive focus towards the supply of additional information in conjunction with the products. The signals of this shift are many. The darling companies of Wall Street today are not Ford and US Steel anymore, but Netscape and Microsoft. Since 1991, investment in the tools of the information era (computers and communication) was higher than capital spending in the industrial sector. By 1992 capital investment in IT was US$25 billion higher already:[7] and the distance between the two is still increasing.

Changes, however, might run even deeper than we have hinted at thus far. Some researchers have suggested that the new economy is based on a totally different principle.

New Economic Laws for the New World

Take a look at any good textbook on economics. In one of the first chapters you are bound to find an explanation of the law of diminishing returns. Very briefly, it states that the more any given resource is used, the smaller is the incremental return. As a consequence of this, the biggest economical advantages come from unexploited, or underexploited resources. This law, while very simple and intuitive, is one of the linchpins of economics, even today, more than one hundred years after it was formulated. Because management theory has its roots in economics, it is only natural that business has accepted the law of diminishing returns, and made it a cornerstone of strategic thinking as well.

What if the law of diminishing returns, at least in some cases, did not apply? What if the more you apply a resource, the more of the same resource is generated and thus the more value that resource creates in the final product? This is what some economists have been trying to find out in recent times, studying what they call positive feedback economics, or new growth economics. According to them, some industries are still regulated by negative feedback mechanism.[8] This means that they are naturally in an equilibrium state, and that as soon as an external occurrence breaks the industry equilibrium, negative feedback cycles will activate, returning the industry to the same or another equilibrium. Expansion of production, for example, will lower price through the spreading of fixed costs over more units of production. However, limited resources available in the world means that the company will have to turn towards lower return ones (land yielding less crop, mining ore that is less pure, financial investments with a lower return, and so on): this will counter the effect of the lower fixed cost quota, and keep the price at a stable level. What is important is that the equilibrium point is single and well determined.

There are some industries that do not react in the same way. In these cases equilibrium points are multiple and it is impossible to forecast which one will emerge as the final equilibrium before the industry actually reaches it. In such cases, if a company manages to break the equilibrium, and gain a slight advantage on competitors, positive feedback loops will amplify this advantage, increasing the lead of the 'deviant' company. It is important to remember that this deviation from equilibrium might be caused by anything at all: superior products or services, added distribution, or random chance events equally.

This is exactly what happened with video recorders and with computer operating systems. In the video recorder industry the VHS and Betamax standards fought for supremacy and were enjoying an almost split market. Then, a series of small events, VHS got slightly ahead of Betamax. Video shops started stocking more VHS tapes than Betamax ones, and video recorder shops had more VHS than Betamax machines. This encouraged customers to go more and more towards the VHS standard, condemning Betamax to extinction in the marketplace. All this happened even though, according to industry experts, Betamax was technically superior to VHS.

Something very similar happened in the computer industry in the beginning of the 1980s. Microsoft's DOS, Apple's Macintosh and CP/M were vying to become the industry standard as operating systems for personal computers. IBM supported DOS and set it as a standard on all its machines. Moreover, IBM licensed the production of compatible machines to other companies (the so-called clone producers), while Apple did not. This ensured that DOS got a wider diffusion, therefore software companies were more inclined to write applications for DOS than for Mac, so customers preferred DOS machines to Mac machines. The result: as of 1996, CP/M is dead, and has been so for many years, due to manifest inferiority; the Mac operating system controls less than 10 per cent of the market, while DOS/Windows holds sway with a market share of over 90 per cent. Once again, industry experts agree that the Mac operating system was much better and easier to use.

According to Brian Arthur,[9] while normal bulk production industries still function according to diminishing returns, high-tech industries are best portrayed through increasing returns.[10] Three main reasons why increasing returns apply to hi-tech products have been identified.

- *Up-front costs.* Increasing return industries usually present very high costs of product development, while the marginal costs of the new products are quite low. This of course means that the average costs will considerably drop as units sold rise.
- *Network effects.* Users must be able to access the product, and that often means that other, related products must be compatible. Products thus have the possibility to lock in the market, that is to become the industry standard and thus to ensure dominance over competitors. Network effects can also materialise in more limited synergies between products compatible with each other.
- *Customer groove-in.* Customers normally need to be trained to use the product, or at least need to get used to it, and are reluctant to switch because of the effort required to get to know another system.

Positive feedback dramatically changes the way the market looks and behaves. The market becomes very unstable. Any small occurrence, which negative feedback would have absorbed, can actually be blown out of proportion and become the factor that makes or breaks a company: remember the slight advantage VHS had over Betamax at the beginning, which turned into total dominance. Companies in this situation cannot afford to play chess games with a long time horizon, conceding battles to win the war. Every battle, in an increasing return industry, is the final one for market dominance, and competitors cannot be allowed to advance even an inch further their current position.

Moreover, forecasts become very difficult if not outright impossible. If small events can totally change the path the industry would take and move companies towards a different equilibrium, then forecasting is akin to crystal ball gazing, because nobody can foresee all the small events that can happen world-wide in a given industry. The rules of the game change as the game develops and unfolds. The rewards, in increasing return markets, will go to the first player to recognise the future shape of the business: ironically enough, then, as forecasting becomes more important, it also becomes more difficult.

Multiple equilibrium points also make optimisation impossible, because optimisation requires the knowledge of the rules and the context of competition. As we said before, this is not the case in increasing returns industries. The only option available to companies is to adapt, and keep on adapting as the world around them changes.[11]

Navigating in the New World

How can management cope with this new business environment? Fast perception of and reaction to changes become essential. The ability to recognise trends and 'see' the future is the key to the continued survival of the company.[12] Management alertness can also be improved through the creation of a leaner organisational structure. This is a trend that we have all witnessed in the past few years. Brian Arthur advocates the transformation of the strategic business units in close-knit commando units, looking for the next big break to exploit.[13] Of course, creating commando units implies more than just eliminating middle management. The units have to be empowered to act with a good level of freedom, thus giving free rein to creativity and innovative solutions.

If slight advantages can be turned into monopoly positions, every battle becomes the crucial one. In such a situation, first-mover advantages become even more important than they normally are. Once a product is locked in, it will take a more superior product to dislodge it from its leading position. For all these reasons, a low price policy during introduction is heavily recommendable. In the mid-1970s Xerox had already introduced a mouse and windows personal computer, but it was priced too high. When Apple came out with the Macintosh, its price was lower than that of its competitors, and this facilitated the introduction of the product.

Customer base gained this way can then also be exploited for other, related products. Microsoft has used this tactic, shifting its strong customer base from DOS, to Windows and Windows 95 systems. It is now trying to exploit this customer base for its Explorer net browser. This 'brand extension' strategy is not always successful, though: the Microsoft Network, presented as an alternative to Internet and America On-line, failed miserably.

Dominance, however, also can be reached through the assistance of other companies operating in other markets. Knowledge-intensive products operate most of the time in close connection with other products. Computer companies need software, peripherals, games; pharmaceutical companies need research labs, hospitals and physicians. Companies therefore operate in mini-ecologies, together with companies and individuals competing in different markets from the main one. At the same time, their support is vital and can spell the difference between a winning and a losing system. Therefore, these 'satellite industries' should be encouraged to cooperate and foster the success of the main products. The slight push they might give the product can be all the company needs to attain the ultimate success.

Psychological positioning, finally, becomes extremely important. If competitors believe that you have locked into the market, they might be reluctant to enter the same market themselves. Product launches, press conferences, early report of new product development, pre-announcements and threatened alliances are all tactics aimed at achieving a psychological edge.

All these suggestions, however, start from a common assumption. The ground-breaking change is that companies have to start to manage all their assets and all their flows, and not just the visible ones. Financial assets are a small part of the company, and a result of something else. In a world where a slight advantage easily turns into a leading position, think about the profits a company correctly utilising all its assets might gain over a company that uses only 20 or 30 per cent of its assets, that is only the financial ones. Thus, managers should learn not to concentrate too much on the visible aspects of the company, just because they are easily recognisable. Like doctors confronted by a disease, managers have to look beyond the surface symptoms and into the deeper causes. Therefore, the real change in store for managers is that they have to start creating a strategy to manage all the intangible value of the company.

The awareness of intellectual capital as something that needs as much attention if not more than financial capital, will force managers to change their whole perspectives of the world. Time delays and intangibility conspire to make intellectual capital strategy even more difficult to plan than the financial capital one. Managers thus have to resort to navigation instead of planning. Abandoning all hope of going straight towards the goals, managers need to learn to set a clear direction and then stay as close to it as they can. It is not an easy task.

In our opinion, it requires a clear understanding of the concept of intellectual capital, as well as the concepts behind it. Building an intellectual capital system in a company with no understanding of the assumptions and origins behind it is akin to building a house on sand. As long as the weather is fine the house will stand, but when the weather takes a turn for the worse, a house built on sand will not be able to withstand the storm. Therefore, we will finish this chapter with a (brief) examination of all the theory that coalesced into intellectual capital, and with a definition of the concept of intellectual capital itself. The purpose of these paragraphs is not to present an academic study of the relevant theory but solid and shared foundations on which to build the concepts and, more importantly, the practice of intellectual capital.

Identifying the Strategy Roots of Intellectual Capital

The problem of the management of knowledge is not new, and there have been other theories that have tried to tackle it. 'Intellectual capital' then is only the latest development of this line of thinking. To be more precise, the theoretical roots of intellectual capital can be traced to two different streams of thought. We will call the two streams the strategic stream and the measurement stream (Figure 1.2). The first one studied the creation and use of knowledge, as well as the relationship between knowledge and success or value creation. The second focused on the need to develop a new information system, measuring non-financial data alongside the traditional financial ones. We will cover the strategy stream in this paragraph, while the measurement stream will be examined in the next. Afterwards, we will show what intellectual capital is, and what it adds to the existing body of theory on knowledge in business.

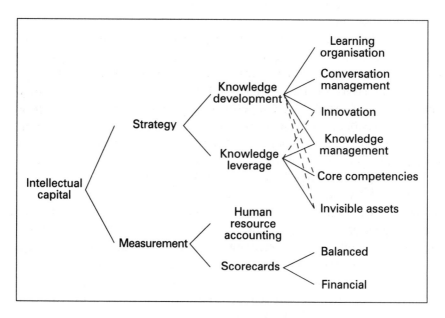

Figure 1.2 Conceptual roots of intellectual capital

Even though they use different names to define it, all the strategic contributions on knowledge[14] look at two main points: the way knowledge is created and the way it is leveraged into value. Some of course are mostly focused on one of these two aspects: the learning organisation, for example, examines mostly the mechanism of knowledge development, while core competencies are concerned mainly with knowledge leveraging. Other concepts are more balanced, focusing on both: knowledge management, for instance, examines equally the development and leveraging sides. Most, however, have at least some elements of both.

Knowledge Development in Companies

A company can develop knowledge in two different ways: through purchase or internal development. Purchase implies the acquisition of a key person, patent or company who possesses or incorporates the knowledge, and then the attempt to spread that knowledge throughout the organisation. This strategy is only apparently easy, because the company can never be sure that the competence acquired is the one the company really needs. Moreover, sharing this competence inside the organisation is not an easy task. It is still a very fast method of acquiring new knowledge, when it works, and can be very effective.

Most of the attention of the literature, however, is given to the internal development of knowledge, through research and development or training. Naturally enough this avenue requires investments too. However, there is no direct correlation between the amount of investment and the results. Some small investments can generate high amounts of knowledge, while some heavy investments can utterly fail to generate any new competence: uncertainty is in-built in research, and even training can be pointless if the subjects consciously or unconsciously refuse to learn.

According to an established classification, knowledge can be either tacit or explicit.[15] While explicit knowledge is codified in written form, tacit knowledge is inside the individual, and cannot be fully explained. Further knowledge is created as knowledge moves from tacit to explicit and back.[16] More specifically, tacit to tacit interactions create knowledge through conversation or reflections. The move from tacit to explicit implies codifying something, thus making it accessible to everybody.[17] Explicit to tacit knowledge transfers instead require somebody to access codified documents and learn from them: reading books or reports is a good example. Finally, the possibility of explicit to explicit transfer is considered. However, as knowledge cannot at present be created either by computers or by books, we do not believe that there can be a direct explicit to explicit knowledge transfer. Explicit to explicit transfers can involve only data: to have knowledge, data must be interpreted by a human mind.

These movements of knowledge along the tacit–explicit spiral are essentially events of knowledge sharing. The problem of knowledge sharing is therefore a crucial one: where there is no knowledge sharing, there is no knowledge creation, because all knowledge resides in the minds of the people of the organisation and it does not move or grow. But how do you get different people in the organisation to share skills and knowledge? The answer is easy: to share knowledge people have to communicate, either orally or through written means. Communication helps the company to make sense of the world, and thus to create the conditions for action. Academics and practitioners alike are discovering the importance of communication and the use of language within companies, and a new field of research on conversation management is growing.[18]

The difficult part is creating an environment where people can communicate. Technical systems can help, but a technical system in itself cannot ensure communications. Office architecture can be designed to create occasions for chance meetings, through open spaces, common rooms and the like. Not even this, however, can create knowledge on its own. Communication, and thus knowledge, can be born only from willing behaviour to share.

So, should we abandon all hope of generating knowledge? No, fortunately enough. Twenty-five centuries ago Aristotle had already remarked that man is a social animal, and history has not changed us much in that respect. We still feel the urge to sit around the campfire and share tales of the hunt: we have simply exchanged the campfire for the water-cooler and the hunt for the newest market strategy. This natural behaviour should be encouraged. Bosses should not reprimand their subordinates because they talk too much: they should encourage them to share opinions on the company's operations and actions, as well as its strategic direction. Discussion and criticism should be encouraged and well received. In this way, suggestions will be generated. Some of them will be stupid, some impractical, but some might just be incredible insights. The loss of structure that comes from this need for a free communication means that control has to move through the social dimension. Managers thus have to become leaders, creating a sharable goal that can focus and guide the organisation.[19] Their task as leaders also becomes one of constructing the best environment and attitude for the creation and diffusion of knowledge. This attitude, it has been observed, comes through the building of trust between the managers and the employees.[20] Only trust can make knowledge flow inside the company, generating a shared world of experience.

Leveraging Knowledge in Companies

Once knowledge has been created, it is of no use if it cannot be applied to the business operations of the company. Knowledge application is the first and foremost aim of any commercial endeavour, as it creates value from the knowledge accumulated in the company, thus (hopefully) enhancing the financial situation of the company itself. Moreover, through experimentation a company learns more, that is creates new knowledge. It is widely recognised that the first versions of computer software and hardware will usually be full of bugs, which are then fixed in subsequent versions.

Application also creates know-how, that is practical knowledge and skills on how to apply the theoretical knowledge, as well as tricks of the trade and practical arrangements. The fact that the best CD player manu- facturers are still Sony and Philips is not only because the technological abilities of these companies are superior to those of their competitors; no, in small part, this market situation is due to the fact that Sony and Philips were the first two companies on the market, and thus have been manufac- turing CD players longer than any other company.

It is important to note there is no definite boundary between knowledge development and knowledge application. The distinction is made purely for the purpose of discussion, but in reality the two activities are very enmeshed. The very roots of our scientific method established by Galileo three centuries ago foster the use of experimentation as a validation of theoretical knowledge.

If we say that application develops knowledge, larger companies have, as a rule, more opportunities to learn than smaller ones. This is obvious: if each and every transaction is a learning occasion, just imagine the poten- tial Procter & Gamble has for learning compared to, say, the local grocer. For this very reason, any company should try to multiply the occasions of knowledge application: offering components as well as finished products, for example, becomes a winning strategy,[21] as does the application of the same competence in multiple markets. The Virgin Group, for example, has managed to use its knowledge of the needs of one particular age group (teenagers to 30-year-olds, more or less) in such different markets as music retailing, music production, airlines, soft drinks, insurance and video games, in all cases with resounding success, and in all cases generating new knowledge.[22]

The ability to apply competencies (as well as the ability to profit from learning occasions) is a skill in itself. Some authors have referred to this, and other similar skills, as meta-skills, meaning that they are skills regulating the creation and deployment of new skills.[23] Learning, knowledge sharing and lateral thinking are all examples of prerequisite skills the company needs to make the most out of its experiences. Meta-skills regulate, among other things, the transformation of potential learning occasions into actual learning occasions. The problem, unfortunately, is that there is no sure-fire way of developing these skills. As we noted above when discussing knowledge development, it all comes down to a question of behaviour.

In conclusion, the suggestions of the strategic thinkers can be summarised as follows:

- Knowledge and learning are key competitive advantages in today's world.
- While information technology, organisational structure and physical layout can help, companies should aim for a behavioural change.
- The development and leveraging of knowledge cannot be separate activities.
- Widespread application of knowledge is a goal in itself and a means to develop new knowledge.

Identifying the Measurement Roots of Intellectual Capital

As we mentioned before, the enormous development of the invisible side of the economy in the 1980s also resulted in a series of contributions from the accounting sciences in tackling the measurement of the invisible side of the economy. Some attempts in this direction had already been made in the 1970s, with the development of human resource accounting but they had failed to generate widespread support. The quest for new performance measures continued in the 1980s, with the advent of the quality movement.[24] Global competition, government regulation and peer pressure[25] were all factors in influencing the growth in the use of quality measures among manufacturers. However, the speed with which managers connected with quality theory is a sign of discontent with the existing focus on financial performance as the yardstick for measurement of the company's health. The pressure for the renovation of measures continued to build up with the tentative development of measures for customer satisfaction.[26]

The watershed in the search for alternative measures came with an article in the *Harvard Business Review* in 1991, by Robert Eccles: 'The performance measurement manifesto'. In it, the author suggested five steps to create a new measurement system:

- Develop a new information architecture.
- Determine the hardware, software and telecommunications technology needed.
- Align the system to the incentives.
- Draw on outside resources and third parties.
- Design a process to ensure the other four activities happen.

The development of the measurement architecture implies agreeing on what kind of data the management needs for its strategy, how these data should be generated and what are the rules regulating their flow. Measurement systems are thus strategy-specific, and could change over time in any company. It is also possible that different divisions in the same company might use different measures. However, some common indicators valid for the whole company should be found, to create a common ground to discuss strategic decisions. The flexibility of measures also helps the company to adapt to any new situation or structure, avoiding the typical problems of measurement and structure pulling the company in different directions.

We also believe in the importance of underlining the role of third parties. Consulting companies, academics, industry associations and regulatory committees will all have a great role (as they actually have had in the past) in determining the new measurement system(s). A company should therefore monitor carefully the movements of these external forces, lest new regulations catch it unawares.

Scorecards – Financial or Balanced?

The call for a new measurement system has been answered, at least indirectly, by the suggestion coming from many sides that a company should adopt not a single measure to guide its decisions, but an assortment of indicators, which could draw a clearer picture of the real situation, and thus be far more useful to the company.[27] Any company is a complex system and trusting only one kind of data to provide enough information to guide it is close to pretending to fly an airplane with only one instrument (either measuring speed, altitude, fuel or pressure, but not more than one at the same time). While most companies agree that a scorecard composed of multiple measures is needed to help the company navigate the new environment, a debate has emerged, arguing whether a balanced approach or a financial approach should be employed in its construction.

Companies like Royal Dutch Shell and Fortis, an American financial services giant, opt for a financial scorecard, arguing that financial measures are the only ones reliable enough to have any meaning.[28] They believe that monitoring many financial measures, as opposed to concentrating on a few, can yield many useful pieces of information to top management, who can then act on them. Royal Dutch Shell itself measures the growth of revenues, the market value of the company, the economic value added and the return on investment, and then collates the data visually in a matrix. This multiple focus, they believe, gives them a balanced view between short-term and long-term profitability and can signal to top management the areas where the company performance should be improved.

In the other camp we have those companies and academics who suggest that financial measures are not enough, that they indicate only the result of the past and thus have no value for the future. Therefore, they conclude, financial measures should be flanked by non-financial measures, monitoring the other success drivers of the company. Cycle times, rate of on-time delivery, repeat business, employee turnover and similar measures can help the company to craft a fuller strategy than bare financial figures ever could. This balanced scorecard can also be used to show financial investors the true value of a company, even though most of the time the diffusion of a scorecard would give away too much about the company's strategy.

The Balanced Scorecard

Robert Kaplan of the Harvard Business School and David Norton of the Renaissance Strategy Group, the initiators of the balanced scorecard movement, suggest creating a scorecard looking at financial, customer, internal and growth measures, to keep a good balance between present and future, and internal and external perspectives.[29] While this structure might be a good framework, the specific indicators chosen should, as

cont'd

Eccles suggested, depend on the strategy, and more precisely on the identified strategic drivers (or key strategic factors). The problem of course is choosing the right measures. Ideally the measures chosen for a balanced scorecard must be:

- affected by the actions of the unit, and by the actions of the unit in question only
- consistent with the short-term and long-term goals of the company
- reliable

It is unlikely that a measure will satisfy all three criteria, and some trade-off will usually be required. It is important, however, for the company to keep all three dimensions in mind when building a balanced scorecard.

Before we conclude the discussion on scorecards, it is interesting to note that whether they are financial or balanced, they should meet the three criteria set out by Eccles which we described above. Scorecards are in fact a new measurement architecture, which should be based on the strategy of the company. The debate on scorecards is heavily influenced by outside forces, mainly academics and the media; even the big six accounting companies are now catching up and joining the fray. As for the technological requirements, the alignment with incentives and the process to realise the system, these are all specific implementation processes which vary from application to application. The theory, though, stresses all three points, so correct application of scorecards should satisfy these criteria as well.

So, should a company use a financial or a balanced scorecard? Characteristics of each approach are summarised in Table 1.3 below. Even though we recognise all its drawbacks, we believe that a balanced approach is preferable. In today's world it is essential to have a clear picture of all the aspects of a company. Going back to the airplane metaphor, using a financial scorecard is like having a lot of information on fuel (level, consumption, pressure, status of the fuel system, and so on) while ignoring all the data on altitude, position and all the other systems in the plane.

Table 1.3   Financial *v.* balanced scorecard

	Financial	*Balanced*
Reliability	High	Medium
Ease of use	High	Low
Comprehensiveness	Low	High
Time and effort required to develop	Low	High
Comparability	Medium	Low

It is also true that the real value of any model is in its power to make people question their normal assumptions, and thus think about what they are doing and how they are doing it.[28] All the same, this rethinking of the basic assumption is much deeper in the case of the balanced scorecard (and thus can be a stimulus to more learning occasions).

In conclusion, measurement systems must evolve to be useful to the twenty-first century enterprise. The evolution is necessary because the data that needs to be tracked today is much more extensive than it has ever been. Some people believe that this evolution can be carried out through a rise in the number of financial measures used. Others, and we count ourselves among this group, believe that a qualitative shift is required towards non-financial measures.

Reporting the Intangible Side of the Company

The drive for measuring the invisible processes and assets of companies has resulted in some instances in the publication of a fully-fledged report, detailing the evolution and the value of these activities. Skandia, the Swedish insurance and financial services company, has been a pioneer in this field, publishing the first report on intellectual capital as a one-page section in its 1993 Annual Report, and then promoting it to a full supplement the following year. Since 1994 Skandia has published an intellectual capital supplement with each year and half-year report.[30] Dow Chemicals followed Skandia's example in 1996 when it published *Visualizing Intellectual Property in Dow*, a report detailing the company's efforts to evaluate and properly use all its intellectual property.

The purpose of these reports, of course, is to give all stakeholders an understanding of what the real value of the company is, and where is it coming from. We have already noted how the excessive focus on financial factors creates a warped image of the company's situation, and it is perfectly understandable that any company would try to draw a truthful representation of itself to all stakeholders.

The forms of these reports are as various as the possible ways to measure/exploit intellectual capital. A company usually reports what it is doing and how, as well as the results of its efforts to improve this invisible side of the company. There are, however, signs in the business world that these reports will become more and more common in the near future. SEC, the American Stock Exchange 'watchdog', has stated that in a few years' time companies quoted on Wall Street will be forced to publish such a report, to integrate the information available to financial markets and investors. The standard format for the reporting is probably going to be that adopted by Skandia.[31] Steven Wallman, SEC commissioner, recently stated:

> I can envision... a very different kind of financial reporting system... [with] the auditor function certifying the information going into a database. You could access the database and create your own kind of financial statement, based on your preferences and the kinds of things you look for. [32]

Intellectual Capital: What's the Difference?

Given the situation we have illustrated, it is not surprising that the two streams tried to converge. What is unusual is that this merging step was taken by practitioners instead of academics: the theoretical debate started after the leading practitioners started talking and publishing about intellectual capital. Even more surprisingly, more companies were working on the same problem at the same time, without knowing of each other's efforts. Thus intellectual capital is the answer to a very practical and widespread need to manage the whole company and not just its visible part, integrating the need for a complete measurement system with the need for a holistic management strategy.

For us, intellectual capital will include all the processes and the assets which are not normally shown on the balance sheet, as well as all the intangible assets which modern accounting methods consider (mainly trademarks, patents and brands). While knowledge is a part of IC, IC is much more than just knowledge. Brands and trademarks as well as the management of relations with external parties (trade distributors, allies, customers, local communities, stakeholders in general and the like) are all dimensions of value creation.

Invisible Assets

The flow of information between the company and the environment, or inside the company creates invisible assets. These assets are semi-fixed (that is they need to be built over a long time period), can be employed for more uses at the same time and are enhanced by increased use. As such, they provide a longer-lasting source for competitive advantage than do financial assets.[33]

One of the first attempts to capture the invisible part of the company is Itami's theorisation of 'invisible assets'. Contrary to invisible assets, intellectual capital is NOT information-based: it is knowledge-based. The distinctions between the two should be clear by now: knowledge is a personal, subjective process emerging from previous experiences and current events, while information is objective data about the environment. The fact that they are knowledge-based, though, actually reinforces the characteristics traditionally associated with invisible assets. Knowledge takes time to build, and so do knowledge-based assets, probably to a greater extent than do information-based assets. Also, we have already noted how knowledge increases with use, through increasing returns.

Core Competence

A core competence is a bundle of constituent skills and technologies, creating disproportionate value for the customer, differentiating its owner from the competitors and allowing entrance to new markets. It is not an asset, but an activity or an accumulation of learning. A core competence is a source of competitive advantage, but not all competitive advantages are core competencies. A core competence usually results in more than one product, and a product can be the result of multiple core competencies.[34]

Core competence, another popular concept studying knowledge and its application, is more restricted in its focus than is intellectual capital. While a core competence is certainly part of IC, IC is much more than core competencies. Core competencies are very limited in scope, as highlighted by the numerous requirements set on a competence to consider it core. IC is much more general, examining both core and non-core competencies, as well as the results of the application of these competencies. The selection of the core versus non-core capabilities are left to the individual managers, much the same as the selection between core versus non-core monetary or physical assets. However, non-core invisible assets or competencies still need to be managed, although of course with relatively less attention.

The Learning Organisation

A very popular stream of theory headed by Peter Senge of the MIT suggests that the key to survival of companies is to become learning organisations, that is systems where an ongoing, continuous and never-ending process of learning is taking place involving all parts of the system itself. To achieve this goal, companies need to master five separate abilities:

- The ability to create a shared vision.
- The ability to share knowledge and thus learn as a team.
- The ability to develop mastery, a behavioral variable stimulating organisational members in the search for further knowledge.
- The ability to elicit, evaluate and change the mental models of the company members.
- System thinking, that is the ability to see events not as a linear chain but as an interconnected web, with systemic and cyclical features.

The most important discipline, according to the author, is system thinking: without that, a company will always be burdened with unforeseen consequences to all its actions.[35]

Learning organisation theory concentrates too much on the development of knowledge and not enough on its exploitation. Thus, while we agree that companies should actively seek any learning occasion and turn it into an increase in the company's intellectual capital, we believe it is important to consider also the exploitation side of the problem. Moreover, Senge and his followers do not consider the possibility of expliciting the knowledge accumulated in the company, while this should be a goal for most of the companies.

Intellectual capital is much more comprehensive, then, than any of the other terms suggested in the literature or practice. The comprehensiveness of IC coupled with its practical origins means that it does not (or not only) aim at understanding the hidden value of the company, nor at visualising and measuring the same. Instead, the goal is to visualise and measure it in order to leverage it and create new value. This, as we said above, is also the goal of the book you hold in your hands. Even though sometimes it might seem that we are being sidetracked into pointless academic discussions, we believe that a little theoretical background can help companies to create a better intellectual capital system, and to manage it more effectively.

We still have not given a definition of intellectual capital, albeit we have indicated what we mean by the term. Let's conclude the chapter, then, with something that comes close to a definition, or, to be more precise, two definitions, a positive and a negative one. The positive one suggests that the intellectual capital of a company is the sum of the knowledge of its members[36] and the practical translation of this knowledge, that is brands, trademarks and processes. The negative definition suggests that intellectual capital is anything that can create value but that you cannot drop on your foot – in other words, it is intangible; that is it is the difference between the total value of the company and its financial value.

New World, New Words

We have seen how the world has changed, and knowledge (or the invisible side of the company) has emerged as the key resource, or at least one of the key resources, of any company. Also, knowledge-intensive companies might actually follow a different economic law: the law of increasing returns. This means that all resources have to be managed in the most efficient way, because a small slip in efficiency can be turned by competitors into a big lead. As such, the invisible assets and processes (which we call intellectual capital) have to be specifically addressed, and a new management logic needs to be developed.

We have, then, examined the origins of the concept of intellectual capital, and the theories on which it is founded. We have also underlined the differences between intellectual capital and these previous theories, and we have concluded the chapter with a new definition of IC. We are now ready to explore the concept of intellectual capital, and to separate its different components.

2 Finding New Words

We are now entering the least exciting chapter of the book. Unfortunately, to create a correct intellectual capital system, we believe it is necessary to understand what are the different categories and flows of intellectual capital: it is just a question of understanding what we are looking at. Trying to create an intellectual capital system without this understanding would be like flying blind and hoping for the best. In a way, if we resume our navigation metaphor, defining the categories and flows of IC is akin to defining the mountains, hills and rivers of the new terrain.

While this may all make perfect sense, and we think it does, long lists of capital forms are certainly not wildly exciting. We have reduced the list to nine forms of intellectual capital, grouped in two more general categories. This still leaves us with 90 possible flows, if we include also the flows to and from financial capital. We will try to make the examination of these categories and flows as interesting as we can, adding examples and limiting the theoretical discussion to a bare minimum. All the same, we cannot guarantee that this chapter will make for an interesting read, although it will certainly be a useful one.

Thus we have two conflicting objectives. On one hand, we firmly believe that it is important to create a common language on intellectual capital, and that means identifying the different stocks and flows. On the other hand, we are perfectly conscious that this identification is not the most exciting topic in the world. All we can do, though, is try to keep the discussion short, and ask the readers to bear with us.

Intellectual Capital: What's In It?

Although we have defined the concept of intellectual capital, the alternative definitions we suggest above are still too general to be of any help in the strategy-making process. What we need to do is to distinguish the different components within this nebulous, all-embracing concept. The identification of these components will, hopefully, help to improve our understanding of what intellectual capital is, and will also enable us to take the concept down to a strategic and even operational level. Hence, it will be possible, in the next chapters, to develop appropriate techniques for measuring IC.[1]

The Skandia Model

Skandia divides market value into financial capital and intellectual capital (Figure 2.1). Intellectual capital is further divided into structural capital (defined as what remains in the company when the people go home: brands, trademarks, written procedures for processes, and so on) and human capital (anything that thinks). Structural capital includes customer and organisational capital, representing the external and internal focus, respectively, of structural capital. Organisational capital consists of innovation and process capital. Process capital is the sum of know-how that is formalised inside the company: manuals, best practices, intranet resources, project libraries are all part of the project capital. Innovation capital is what creates the success of tomorrow: it is the source of renewal for the whole company, and it includes intellectual assets and intellectual property.

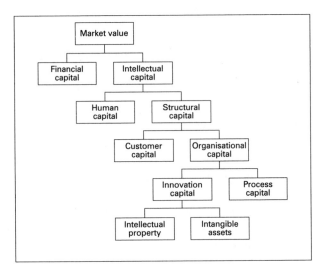

Figure 2.1   The Skandia Value Scheme

SOURCE: Skandia (1996)

Our categories will be based on the pioneering work of Skandia. Starting from the balanced scorecard approach, Skandia practically single-handedly started the intellectual capital movement, in 1994, through the publication of an Intellectual Capital Report as a supplement to its Annual Reports. We will build on Skandia's basic, adding more branches and refining the categories further.

First, we need to backtrack and specify something that has remained implicit until now: the total value of the company can be divided into financial capital and intellectual capital (Figure 2.2). Financial capital includes all the physical and monetary assets, while intellectual capital is made up of all the invisible processes and assets of the company.

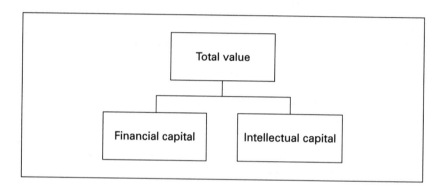

Figure 2.2   Financial *v.* Intellectual Capital

In this book, we shall not devote much space to financial capital. For our purposes, suffice it to say that value from financial capital can come from either the physical or the monetary assets of the company (Figure 2.3).[3] Moreover, we will consider the value of financial capital to equal the replacement value of the company's asset, thus following Tobin's suggestions.[4] This way, the assessment of financial capital becomes less dependent on accounting practices, which vary from company to company and from country to country.

Let's concentrate instead on what intellectual capital consists of (Figure 2.4). If we take a step further and try to create a new distinction, we can divide IC into structural capital and human capital. These two parameters represent what we called before the invisible assets (and the processes, we will add now), and the knowledge embodied in the employees of the company. The separation between 'thinking' and 'non-thinking' intellectual capital can be considered the criterion of distinction at this level.[5] The reason behind this distinction is obvious. People, and thus human capital, need totally different management methods from structural capital. We are going to examine each form of capital in detail in the next two paragraphs. To clear up the differences between our model and some of the others suggested, however, we will also briefly examine the next level of distinction.

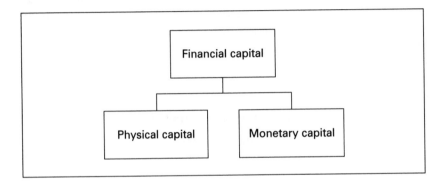

Figure 2.3 Financial Capital

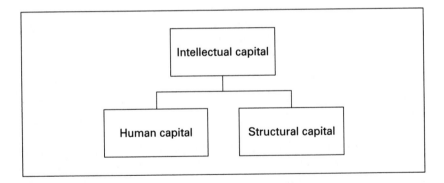

Figure 2.4 Intellectual Capital

Structural capital comes from relationship and organisational value, reflecting the external and internal foci of the company, plus renewal and development value, that is the potential for the future. Value can be generated by all (good) relations with other participants in the environment external to the company,[6] such as its customers, suppliers and alliance partners. Structural and systemic variables that enable the company to perform its daily tasks, for example, its routines and processes, can also generate considerable value.

People generate capital for the company through their competence, their attitude and their intellectual agility. Competence includes skills and education, while attitude covers the behavioural component of the employees' work. Intellectual agility is the ability to innovate and change practices, to think laterally about problems and come up with new and innovative solutions. The distinction of intellectual agility from competence and behaviour is justified by the fact that it is neither a skill nor a behaviour, but a mix of both.

The Three-way Distinction

Most intellectual capital models assume a three-way distinction between:

- external structure
- internal structure
- employees

This distinction, in particular, is suggested by Karl-Erik Sveiby of the University of Queensland,[7] Hubert St Onge formerly of the Canadian Imperial Bank of Commerce[8] and Nick Bontis of the University of Western Ontario,[9] although they use different terms with slightly different meanings to identify the three categories. Bontis and St Onge also emphasise the contribution of tacit knowledge, which they identify as the source of most IC.

Our distinction (and Skandia's) is very similar to the three-way categorisation supported by Karl-Erik Sveiby, Nick Bontis and Hubert St Onge. Human beings, organisational structure and external relations have been identified as the repositories for intellectual capital. But whereas the three-way distinction puts human competence, external structure and internal structure at the same level, we prefer to consider them as two separate levels, introducing structural capital as an aggregation of the two structural variables. This way, the distinction between 'thinking' intellectual capital and 'non-thinking' intellectual capital is clearer and more definite, and we believe that this is the key distinction when it comes to devising the management style required. Moreover, the three-way distinction ignores renewal capital, and thus risks fostering short-termism in managers.

However, unlike Bontis and St Onge, who regard tacit knowledge as the primary source of IC, our classification reduces its contribution. There is no doubt that tacit knowledge plays a key role in the success of the company but care should be taken to avoid overemphasising its merits. Explicit knowledge, in the form of manuals and databases, has created in many cases considerable advantages to companies, enabling management to implement strategies which would have been impossible to realise without this explicit knowledge component. We believe therefore, that the contributions of tacit and explicit knowledge are, if not perfectly balanced, then nearly so. These considerations, however, serve to remind us that the measurement of intellectual capital might be even harder than we thought before. If it is true that tacit knowledge has the lion's share of the merits of IC, then not only is IC intangible, it is also inexpressible!

Annie Brooking/The Technology Broker

Another, slightly different distinction, has been suggested by Annie Brooking of The Technology Broker.[10] According to her, intellectual capital is formed by:

- Market assets: all market related intangibles, including brands, customers, customer loyalty, distribution channels, backlog, and so on.
- Human-centred assets: skills and expertise, problem-solving abilities, leadership styles and abilities and everything that is embodied by the employees.
- Intellectual property assets: know-how, trademarks and patents, and any intangible which can be protected by copyright.
- Infrastructure assets: all the technologies, processes and methodologies enabling a company to function.

The differences between our model and Annie Brooking's are instead more marked. The four components Brooking identifies are indeed important for intellectual capital. However, we believe that they represent different levels of aggregation. We can easily identify the 'people' and the 'external' aspects of IC in, respectively, the human-centred and the market assets. Brooking, however, separates the 'internal' aspect of IC into two parts: infrastructure and intellectual property (IP). This underlining of IP is consistent with her focus on high-tech companies. However, we do not believe that IP warrants a separate consideration, and instead we think that it is part of the organisational structure, as highlighted by the fact that it even shows up in the balance sheet.

Having cleared up our relationship with previous attempts to tackle the issue, we will now proceed in our examination of all the forms of intellectual capital. After a definition of each form and examples of its application, we will also mention what we think are the main components of the form in question. The list is by no means exhaustive, and represents our experience both in practical findings during application of the concepts and theoretical discussions with colleagues. To summarise what we have said so far, we believe that intellectual capital is composed of (and generated by) a thinking part (the human capital) and a non-thinking part (structural capital). We have then suggested that structural capital has an internal and an external component (organisational and relationship capital respectively), while human capital comes from the knowledge, the attitude and the intellectual agility of employees.

The Soul of the Company: Human Capital

There are many stories about how much the stock price dropped when an important individual left the company. Examples like the 10.1 per cent drop in share price after Saatchi & Saatchi announced that its chairman and co-founder Maurice Saatchi was resigning shows how important human resources can be to companies, but it also tells us that human capital is not owned by the company. All employees participate in the company of their own free will. This means that a part of the company's value (and sometimes a big part of it) is not under its direct control. Thus, the company must do all it can to retain all 'good' employees. While this problem has been clear for some time now to managers all over the world, intellectual capital has the merit of showing the issue in simple terms. Bertelsmann, the German media group, has been particularly active in its policies of retention of human capital. This company has taken the concept of profit-related pay one step further, distributing profits in the form of bonds. This way, the profits remain available to the company for reinvestment, but at the same time they are a remuneration for employees, both in terms of interest paid and in terms of the actual value of the profit bond.[11]

Consideration of human capital also sheds new light on training and human resource management policies. If the company can manage to minimise employee turnover, then a heavy investment in training or the development of employees (through social or personal activities) does not only make business sense, it is highly recommendable. The long-term payoffs these investments necessarily imply have, nonetheless, often been a barrier to their spreading. Human capital allows managers to see where all these investments are paying off in the short term.

As we briefly mentioned before, we are going to propose a further subdivision of human capital. We believe that the value of human capital originates from competence, attitude and intellectual agility (Figure 2.5). Each of these components will be examined in turn.

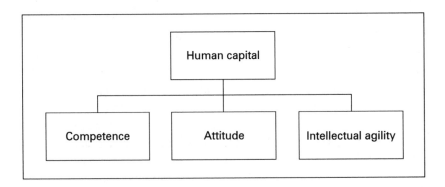

Figure 2.5 Human capital

The Abilities: Competence

Competence generates value through the knowledge, skills, talents and know-how of employees.[12] You could almost say that competencies are the 'content' part of human capital, the hard part.[13] In many ways, it also represents what the organisation can do, its innermost potential, thanks to its employees.[14] As such, we believe that the main components of competence are knowledge and skills (Figure 2.6)

Knowledge, in this classification, indicates the technical or academic knowledge of things.[15] It is generally related to the level of education of a person. Knowledge, in fact, is something that has to be taught. It does not necessarily have to be taught in schools or universities (on-the-field training is totally acceptable), but it still has to be taught. Therefore, knowledge cannot be in-born, and it cannot be increased through learning-by-doing or trial-and-error methods. It needs some kind of learning from books or teachers or mentors. Knowledge does not need to be academic: numismatic experts have a deep knowledge of numismatics, even though numismatics is hardly a university subject.

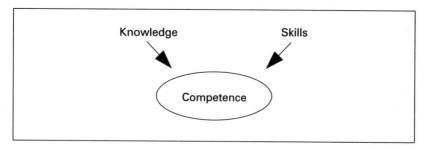

Figure 2.6 Competence

Where knowledge covers the theoretical side, skills are its practical counterpart.[16] By no means less important, skills are obviously related to knowledge, but only distantly: a person with high knowledge can have very low skills, that is can be absolutely unable to tackle a practical application of that knowledge. A typical example of separation between knowledge and skills is computer use. Nowadays, most people know how to use a computer and use one daily: their skills in computer science are high. Not so many, however, could explain how computers work or be able (given the appropriate tools) to build one: they do not have knowledge in computer science. Even without resorting to hi-tech examples, how many people know how a television works precisely? Or a car, for that matter? All the same, as knowledge is increased, usually skills are increased as well. Know-how can be taught and learned, but it might also come from practical experience, whereas knowledge can not.

Competence: Examples of Indicators

- Percentage of company employees holding an advanced degree
- IT literacy
- Hours of training per employee
- Average duration of employment

The Behaviour: Attitude

Knowledge and skills are not everything. Companies need employees who are capable and willing to use their skills and abilities to the advantage of the company and who can motivate the whole company to reach the set goals. What would The Virgin Group be without Richard Branson? Branson's value lies not in his escapades, though Virgin is very good in exploiting them for all they are worth.[17] Nor is it just in his management abilities, even though he managed to become a billionaire by his late twenties. It is most of all in Branson's ability to chart a clear direction for the whole group, and then motivate his employees to reach the goals, no matter what the obstacles are. It is in his ability to be a leader.

Attitude, therefore, is a 'soft' component. The company has very little impact on this side of intellectual capital: attitude depends mostly on personality traits and therefore can be improved very little by company efforts. Some change is possible, however, and can be encouraged through the environment. Attitude is very important for some companies. McKinsey and Procter & Gamble, for example, believe that attitude is at least as important as competence, and both have been known to hire university graduates with non-specialist degrees (architecture, physics or humanities, for example) and give them specific training afterwards: thus, they select an attitude in the candidates and then create the competencies.

Attitude, therefore, covers the value generated by the behaviour of the employees on the workplace. Three factors primarily influence attitude: motivation, behaviour and conduct (Figure 2.7).

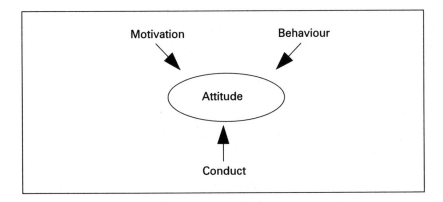

Figure 2.7 Attitude

The ability to reach strategic goals, triumphing over seemingly insurmountable odds, to create the future that one has imagined, to prove that common wisdom is wrong and that the impossible can be done: all this is motivation. Motivation implies falling but always getting up afterwards, having learned from one own's mistake. This ability (we can almost call it stubbornness) has been identified by many researchers and practitioners, and called different names: vision[18] and strategic intent[19] are the most widespread, but by no means the only ones.

The fact that motivation is essential has been repeated so often that it is almost a truism. It is true, though, that many companies seem to have succeeded only on their strength of will and on their commitment to the goals. Komatsu has managed to change from a small local licensee for the production of front-loaders for the construction industry into the world number one producer of earth-moving equipment (at least for a while), through constant, mantra-like repetition of: 'Encircle Caterpillar'.

The most apparent example of this envisioning capability, however, is Swatch. The company, a joint effort by all major Swiss watch manufacturers, tried its first product launch of a bright, cheap watch in the USA, in the late 1970s. The product failed miserably on the market but top management were convinced that this was the right way to answer the challenge posed by the Japanese producers. They therefore persisted, refining the concept and changing the distribution from supermarkets to jewellers (the traditional avenue for watches). As everyone now knows, their motivation has paid off handsomely.

Another factor of attitude is behaviour, encompassing all the value coming from the behaviour of employees in the workplace. Enthusiastic people create dynamic environments, and it has been demonstrated that in such environments everybody seems to be more productive. The value of behaviour is in the creation of the environment that management deems most appropriate.[20] This may happen only if the behaviour required of and obtained from employees is consistent over time.

Skandia has coined a new term that is relevant to behaviour: contactivity. According to the company, contactivity is a meeting that creates contact and activity, and thus, we add, a venue for behaviour to manifest itself. According to the Swedish insurer, contactivity is essential to liberate the energy inside all employees, and to harness that energy to build the future. To create these kinds of meeting Skandia has created new structures, the Future Centers, built to enable different people inside the organisation to come together and share their views of the future and their interpretations of the present.

Behaviour indicates the value coming from the correct behaviour in a strategic perspective: conduct, on the other hand, assumes an ethical perspective, and judges the behaviour not from the standpoint of the future success of the company but from the point of the ethical values of the society the company is operating in. The company can therefore influence conduct capital very little, because it depends on external value judgments. All the same, conduct is important as a generator of value, as evidenced by the bad publicity surrounding companies with consistently reprehensible conduct.

Attitude: Examples of Indicators

- Hours spent in debriefing
- Hours spent by senior staff to explain strategy and actions
- Leadership index
- Motivation index

The Wits: Intellectual Agility

In a fast changing world like ours, the ability to apply knowledge in very different situations, as well as the ability to innovate and transform ideas in products, is crucial to the success of a company. Intellectual agility indicates the ability to transfer knowledge from one context to another, the ability to see common factors in two distinct pieces of information and link them together, and the ability to improve both knowledge and company output through innovation and adaptation.

Intellectual agility can also be a source of successful diversification. The Virgin Group, for example, has reached success through the application of their special knowledge of the teenager to 30-year-old market in industries as diverse as airlines, music and financial products. Similarly, Philip Morris has achieved good results by the cross application in its three main markets (food, beer and cigarettes) of its ability to market high-volume, low-cost items to a large selection of consumers.

Intellectual agility is tightly linked to competence, more so than attitude is. If competence is the content, intellectual agility is the ability to use the knowledge and skills, building on it, applying it in practical contexts and increasing it through learning.[21] Behaviour, on the other hand, relates to the ability to create a climate conducive to the development of intellectual capital in general. Examples of intellectual agility can be innovation, imitation, adaptation and 'packaging' (Figure 2.8).

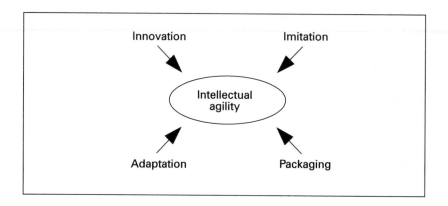

Figure 2.8   Intellectual agility

We define innovation as the ability to build on previous knowledge and generate new knowledge. This ability is fundamental for the renewal of the company, in turn a key event for the creation of sustainable success. Innovation capital covers the individual ability to absorb the existing body of knowledge and know-how, and to increase it. This increase may come from additional insights and categorisation, or through a fundamental rethinking of the matter, causing a paradigm shift. Innovation does not necessarily relate to research and development, even though successful research and development entails innovation. Know-how, however, can be improved through innovation, as can beliefs on the market and competition. Therefore, 3M is a company with a high innovation level, while Apple is not, even though the computer company has the highest R&D budget in the industry.

While innovation is the ability to try something totally new, imitation is the ability to look around, perceive innovation in other industries, fields of activity and companies and then apply it to one's own situation. In everyday language, imitation has a negative connotation because it suggests an inability to innovate. However, not everything that comes out of imitation is of inferior quality to that deriving from innovation. In imitating, companies are also forced to rethink the object of the innovation, to apply it appropriately to their own reality. Thus, they often create something new, showing that the boundaries between imitation and innovation are narrow indeed. Cross-fertilization is another example of the usefulness of imitation. The application of chaos theory (developed in the disciplines of mathematics and physics) to management science and economics is having far-reaching effects.[22]

A company might also try to apply its solutions in a different context, through adaptation. Take Sencorp, for example: the company started out in industrial fastening, and then branched out into wound closure and finally into industrial leasing. Sencorp thus took the experience it had developed in the industrial fastening business and applied to a seemingly unrelated business (wound closure), with a great deal of success. This is an example of a company's successful adaptation to its new environment. The adaptation may become necessary due to a change in the competitive rules (because of a change in technology, a new entrant, new government regulations, a shift in customer tastes, and so on), or because the company is for some reason exploring new territory.

Adaptation can be reactive, if the company waits until it is compelled to change operations. Alternatively, the company can try to anticipate future changes, through financial forecasting, scenario planning or any other forecasting technique. Finally, the company might try to create the change through the enacting of an idea.[23] Sony, for example, decided to go ahead with the Walkman even though the consumer test results suggested that scrapping the project would be the best alternative. In this sense, it could be argued that they imposed a product on the market. The ability to enact changes most often goes hand in hand with a strong organisational motivation because a company needs a high motivation to be able to create a shift in the whole market.

Packaging indicates the ability to turn an idea into a product or service. As such, one could almost say that packaging capital represents the link between human capital and structural capital or financial capital, because it is the ability to turn an idea into something concrete, whether that takes the form of manuals or description, a product or a service. Packaging generates value through a mix of creativity and business sense, the mark of the true entrepreneur.

Intellectual Agility: Examples of Indicators

- Savings from implemented suggestions from employees
- New solutions/products/processes suggested
- Background variety index (individual and group level)
- Company diversification index

What the Company Owns: Structural Capital

We have exhausted the subject of human capital, hopefully without exhausting the readers too much. Bear with us, we are almost halfway through. We now turn towards the second component of intellectual capital: structural capital. In general, structural capital includes all databases, organisational charts, process manuals and intellectual property, and anything whose value to the company is higher than its material value. Skandia defines structural capital as all intellectual capital that remains in the company when employees go home for the night. While this might look like a very general definition, it captures the basic characteristic of the issue.

First of all, structural capital can be, and usually is, owned by the company, as opposed, as we have seen above, to human capital. Mailing lists are proprietary information, processes and breakthrough inventions can be patented, and organisational culture is hardly replicable. Ownership of relationships is a slightly more complicated subject, but usually relationships are with the company as a whole, and not with single individuals inside the company.[24] At the same time, and this is the flip side of the coin, the fact that structural capital is not in anybody's head necessarily implies that its evolution will be much slower than that of human capital. People increase or modify their capital just by living their lives: structural capital, in most cases, needs to be updated by the employees themselves.

Thus, structural capital is (though in varying degrees) proprietary and not self-renewing. Companies therefore have to balance a difficult trade-off between the two kinds of capital. To examine the structural capital in more detail, we will have to distinguish between its different components, as outlined in Figure 2.9.

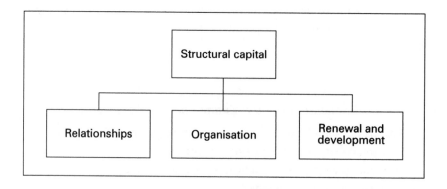

Figure 2.9 Structural capital

The External Actors: Relationships

The downsizing wave and the increased interconnection of previously separate markets and industries are creating the need to rely on external actors even in day-to-day operation. The trend to cost-cutting has led many companies to outsource activities which were once considered essential. For example, what is Nike famous for? Shoes. What does Nike do? It is tempting to answer: 'It produces shoes'. Unfortunately, it is also very wrong. Nike does not directly take part in any of the actual production phases, but limits its activities to planning, product design and development, distribution and marketing activities.

The importance of relationships with outside parties is forcing companies to lengthen their time horizon: relationships are not built through spot transaction, but through long-term exchanges of information and goods.[25] The rewards for this stronger effort are considerable cost-savings (BP reported a saving of £50 million, 30 per cent of the budget, on an offshore project, due to higher cooperation with suppliers[26]) and the possibility of instituting just-in-time policies, as well as, very often, higher quality output through higher quality in the components. Honda has built its success partly on its ability to have dedicated suppliers who were willing to learn with the company.

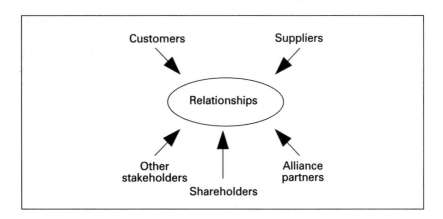

Figure 2.10 Relationships

Unfortunately, all these and other fundamental relationships do not show up in the reporting system currently used as a standard by the companies. How, then, does a firm signify to shareholders that it is a sound investment, insofar as it has loyal clients, is well regarded in financial markets, the local community thinks highly of it and it has long-term alliances with key suppliers and competence holders? To answer all these questions it is necessary to resort to relationship measurements. In our opinion, the most important sources of relationship capital are customers, suppliers, allies, shareholders and other stakeholders (Figure 2.10).

It is common knowledge that gaining a sale with a new customer is much more expensive (one estimate puts it as high as 20 times as expensive[27]) than gaining the same sale with an existing client. Claes Fornell, of the University of Michigan, suggests that customer satisfaction (that is, relationship value originating from the customer) can increase the life expectancy of the relationship, reduce price elasticity, reduce the efficiency of the competitors' effort, lower the cost of attracting new custom and enhance the reputation of the firm.[28] It is quite obvious, then, that the ability of a company to retain customers is essential to its long-term profitability. The creation of a loyal customer base can also be exploited in the case of brand extension, where customers are naturally prone to trust the brand name and try out the new product. Microsoft has used the trick: when launching its Mail application, it specifically targeted the users of the Office suite of applications through added compatibility, special features and discounts.

With the recent orientation towards a greater focus on the core competencies of the firm, reliance on external parties for important parts of the 'supply and demand chain' process has increased considerably. Suppliers are now in many cases considered an integral part of the business system of the company. It is not uncommon today to find employees of the supplier based in the client's headquarters: this has always been common practice in the aircraft industry, but it has become common today even between retailers and mass product producers. Nestlé, for example, has a full-time employee at the central offices of Casino, one of the leading French retailers.[26] These new relationships aim at both reducing costs (through co-marketing, joint training and similar activities) and enhancing the value for both companies. The cooperation can in fact show possible improvements of the product/service offered. To develop closer (and better) relationships, companies are resorting more and more to mono-client supply relationships. As a consequence, competition is now often chain versus chain, and no longer company versus company.

Alliances are becoming the linchpin of many corporate strategies today. Hardly a day passes without two or more companies announcing an alliance of one kind or another. The alliances between British Airways and American Airlines and between British Telecom and MCI are only the most recent examples in a world where choosing the right partners is going to be a key ability. Alliances can have different degrees of formalisation, from official joint venture or any other type of agreement to handshakes and long-term supply relationship which do not need anything written. Some analysts even argue that Intel and Microsoft are *de facto* allies (the so-called Wintel consortium[29]), because their products work one off the other. Cooperation can be started with competitors (to develop a new product: for example the Bell–McDonnell Douglas agreement to develop a light combat helicopter for the US government) or between suppliers and clients (the Motorola–Apple agreement for microprocessors), as we have seen above.

Shareholders can obviously, if push comes to shove, throw a monkey wrench in the best laid management plans. It is therefore a great advantage for the company and management to keep good relations with the shareholders, making sure that management decisions get their approval. Disney shareholders recently made the front page when they protested over the company chairman's remuneration package, and over the severance package for Michael Ovitz, who had been at Disney for only a few months but left with more than US$100 million in severance pay. Although the protest did not have any result, the fact that the *Financial Times* and all the other financial newspapers dedicated their front pages to the news is an indicator of the importance that shareholders have in today's world.

Stakeholders are also becoming more and more aware of their power, and are resorting to loud complaints to protest about the company's actions, thus influencing the company towards more advantageous behaviour. Stakeholder actions can have great consequences on the operations of the company, as the recent boycott of Shell petrol by German consumers over the company's support of the Nigerian government showed. Stakeholder relations can be the hardest form of relations to build up, because most company actions are bound to displease one or another interest group orbiting around the company. Once there, however, they can be a very powerful weapon indeed in achieving the company's strategy. Legends abound about workers suggesting pay cuts in times of trouble, local people pitching in to rebuild the company after natural disasters and governments financing the company expansion or strongly favouring it.

Relationships: Examples of Indicators

- Percentage of supplier/customer business the company accounts for
- Length of relationship
- Partner satisfaction index
- Customer retention

Internal Efficiency: Organisation

With organisational value we come to a form of intellectual capital that is almost totally proprietary, but also totally non-self-replenishing. If this was partly true of relationships, it becomes much more so with organisational value. New relationships can be born from existing ones, with no active effort on the part of the organisational members, thus showing a limited degree of self-renewal; organisational value on the other hand needs constant care and nurturing. At the same time, being proprietary, organisational value is the one most easily visualised and considered. First of all, in most cases organisational capital can be sold or licensed:[30] this gives managers a market value, however approximate, by which to evaluate the structural capital. Moreover, as it affects the daily operations of the company, structural capital has the highest visibility. As a result, most attempts to consider the invisible side of the company in the past have focused on organisational value.

Organisational value includes all the physical and non-physical manifestations of intellectual capital related to the internal structure or the day-to-day operations. Databases, process manuals, invisible assets, culture and management styles are all sources of organisational value. Also, organisational value is usually the result of the effort of a company to turn human capital in proprietary information, and to share that information among all employees. Internal networks thus are part of this category of capital.

As this is the most visible part of intellectual capital, many companies have already started systematically to tackle the issue of nurturing organisational value. Knowledge management programmes have focused on the creation of databases to share best practices and to map the competencies of the organisation and its members – like Arthur Andersen has done with its AA On-line;[31] countless books have remarked on the importance of culture in the achievement of success;[32] and the role of processes has been suitably highlighted.[33] We will thus build on these previous efforts and organise it in our own intellectual capital framework. In particular, we will concentrate on three different aspects of the organisation capital: infrastructure, processes and culture (Figure 2.11).

Arthur Andersen

At the beginning of the 1990s Arthur Andersen started a huge internal project to try to capture the knowledge that the organisation had developed in its consultancy practice. The first outcome, in July 1992, was a CD-ROM on Global Best Practices (GBP) containing 2000 pages of text which described ten established consultancy processes. The company soon realised, however, that the information was useless because it did not have adequate support and navigation to go with it: consultants all over the world did not know how to make use of those 2000 pages. The company's solution was to improve the navigation tools of the CD and the explanation/support structure (creating, for example, a hotline to answer questions, as well as presenting it to subsidiaries all over the world instead of just sending it). They also created another on-line database, called AA On-line, which enclosed personal information on each and every consultant in Arthur Andersen, their competence and their specialities, as well as practical, hands-on tips and comments on established practices.

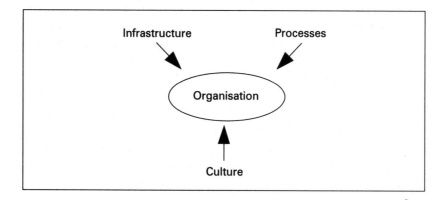

Figure 2.11 Organisation

Infrastructure identifies all the value coming from the structural layout of the organisation, as well as from all the intellectual property assets of the company (patents, trademarks, brands and so on). As such, it represents the hardware part, the tools and enablers the company uses in its daily operations to produce results. The perfect infrastructure would be flexible enough to co-evolve with its environment, connecting employees at all levels (facilitating information sharing) and being extremely replicable, to enhance connectivity and save costs.

An important part of the company's intellectual capital infrastructure is intellectual property, that is the sum of the patents, trademarks, brands, special designs and processes whose ownership is granted to the company by law. Beside these traditional elements, in recent years companies have seen other, more unconventional ones enter into the intellectual property category: mailing lists, customer databases and process manuals, for example, are all granted legal protection against competitors. Dow Chemicals is a leading company in the correct evaluation of the traditional side of intellectual property.[34]

Dow Chemicals

In a programme to catalogue all their intellectual property so as to use it better in their day-to-day operations, Dow Chemicals created a discrete Intellectual Asset function. This function started in 1993 to make order among the patents of the company (more than 29 000). In three years all the patents were categorised and a complete structure was in place to understand the value of the patents and to develop a consistent strategy for their use. Individual patents have also been classified according to their strategic importance to the company. Over 30 per cent of the patents were found to be rarely, if ever, used by the company and have been abandoned, although the function did try to salvage some value out of them through donations to universities and non-profit organisations. All these efforts have suggested the setting of a licensing target for the year 2000 of US$125 million, five times the licensing revenues in 1994.[35]

If the infrastructure is the hardware, processes are the software, that is the operations that make the organisation tick. The perfect structure would be absolutely useless if nobody knew how to put that structure to work. Processes and procedures are normally transmitted through oral tradition, but there have been numerous cases of companies formalising them in documents and manuals.

Processes are what makes it all come together. Any activity inside the company is a process and contributes to the creation of organisation capital. The consequence of this consideration is that processes are extremely varied. The trick is to have the whole organisation share the learning that comes from each process: the problem is that, given the variability of processes, learning methods can be established only on a case-by-case basis. The creation of databases for best practices, for example, is nothing other than the transformation of process capital into infrastructure capital, allowing the company to replicate the specific process when needed.[35] In 1995 American Skandia created the position of the Learning Controller, whose task is to ensure that process capital is transformed into infrastructure.[36] Chevron, on the other hand, has started sharing best practices through a global programme that addresses the issue of best (and good) practices.

Chevron

Realising that different plants often carried out the same procedures in widely differing ways, Chevron has recently started a company-wide effort to share best practices in an attempt to improve efficiency. In their definitions, there are four different levels of best practices: industry best practices, local best practices, good practices and good ideas. The last two levels are sometimes overlooked because they are not the best you can have; nonetheless, they can often generate considerable savings. Sharing at all levels of practices is encouraged. Practically, the company regulates all strategic, high impact practices, prescribing the best one to use. Employees, though, are also encouraged to look for good ideas in their day-to-day operations, and this creates a grassroots approach. Databases and IT networks are used to circulate ideas and process descriptions throughout the company.

The company estimates that this best practice effort saves them US$130 million per year in energy utilisation, and since 1992 has reduced annual operating expenses by US$1.6 billion and downstream capital projects cost by US$530 million. Also, they value the culture that the effort has created: Chevron is now readier than ever to see learning from others as a source of competitive advantage.

We will now consider the culture aspect of organisational value. This is the soft, evolving part and it is tempting to call it the 'wetware' of organisational capital. It is a series of rites, symbols and norms that define the organisation as much as its physical counterparts (headquarters, logos, products and everything else). Culture is created by the constant interactions of organisational members,[37] and the longer those interactions are the stronger is the culture. Culture is important in providing organisational members with a framework in which to interpret events. To avoid overloading of information, this common framework helps group members in selecting the relevant events. Culture can influence the management style (creating a social norm for managers to follow) and the motivation of its employees, through continuous encouragement to strive for the organisational goals.

The Forms of Capital

Vincenzo Perrone, of Università Bocconi, has distinguished between:

- Financial capital: the traditional items present in the financial statements.
- Cultural capital: the value of all the cultural elements of a company.
- Social capital: the value of the network of relations the company is in.
- Symbolic capital: the ability of the company to influence perception and sensemaking of other actors.

Although Perrone never mentions intellectual capital, his research starts from the same point as ours, namely the consideration that there is more to the company than its financial capital.[38]

Symbols are a very important part of culture. Symbolic capital is 'the [...] credit a company has in affirming its own vision of reality and its own position in that reality, as the one considered acceptable and legitimate by other players'.[38] Symbolic capital is a mix of recognition and history, used to influence the perception and sensemaking activities of other actors. This form of capital originates from the company's ability to craft a vision of reality powerful enough to be accepted by employees, customers, suppliers and competitors alike. It is the result of individual and organisational motivation, as well as a cognitive activity in the creation of metaphors and symbols.

Unlike Perrone, we will not consider symbolic capital to be a basic component of intellectual capital, although we still recognise its power. In our opinion, symbols are an integral part of culture, especially when it comes to the recommendations for its management. Also, we consider it as an element within organisational capital, while Perrone believes that it is a special type of social capital. While it is true that symbols unfold all their value in the relationships the company has with outsiders, we believe that this value is much more powerful with respect the internal relationships than external ones. Furthermore, symbolic capital is a result of the climate and culture of an organisation, and thus has an internal origin, as opposed to one connected with relationships that start out as external.

Organisation: Examples of Indicators

- Administrative expenses/total revenues
- Revenues from patents
- Processes completed without error
- Cycle/process time

The Future: Renewal and Development Value

The last category of structural capital is renewal and development value. This includes the intangible side of anything and everything that can generate value in the future, through an improvement of financial and intellectual capital. Thus, investments in new plants and machines are part of renewal and development value as long as they are in the planning phases, but become financial assets when they get to realisation. Similarly, investments in training employees can be included in renewal and development capital only as far as the planning stages: afterwards, they become a flow of financial capital to human capital.

In a way, renewal and development capital includes all the items that have been built or created and that will have an impact on future value, but have not manifested that impact yet. New product development, re-engineering and restructuring efforts, development of new training programmes, research and development are all examples of renewal and development value. It is possible to say, therefore, that this category is a value manifestation of the time delays occurring. Projects are part of renewal and development value only as far as their realisation: afterwards, they become new value of the chosen form.

The challenge for managers, of course, is to balance the need for investments in the future with the condition of short-term survival and prosperity. Management should therefore strive to create a renewal strategy that is consistent with the present situation of the company, the future as the company envisions it and the goals the company has set itself.

Renewal and Development: Examples of Indicators

- Percentage of business from new products
- Training efforts (both in expense per employee and hours per employee)
- Renewal expenses/operating expenses
- New patents filed

The Flows of Intellectual Capital

We have (at long last, you are probably saying!) finished our explorations of the forms of capital. Most of the other authors we have examined in the boxes above have stopped at this point, considering the task of research over with the correct identification of the different forms of capital.[40] This is what has prompted Karl-Erik Sveiby, however, to write that intellectual capital theory has so far focused on the static properties of knowledge.[41] Let's try to apply the same line of reasoning to traditional accounting. Examining only the stocks of capital is akin to using only the balance sheet to plan the future strategy of the company. Now, while nobody denies that the balance sheet is important, and indeed fundamental, using only that and forgetting about all other financial reporting tools (such as the profit and loss statement or the sources and uses of fund statement) would be deleterious in the best case, disastrous in the worst.

Balance sheets are snapshots in time but tell us absolutely nothing of all the events between any two. As our purpose is to help to manage intellectual capital, this 'snapshot' approach does not seem appropriate, leaving out, as it does, all explanations as to why the situation is like it is and where the results come from. To understand these changes in the stocks of capital it is essential to examine the flows of capital, that is the transformation of intellectual capital into financial capital and vice versa, and the internal flows of intellectual capital (Figure 2.12). Only through such an examination, and thus the use of a balance sheet AND a profit and loss approach to IC, can meaningful measures like return on intellectual capital be developed.[42] Remember that our final goal is to create a system which will help companies to monitor efficiency of the intangible part of the company; you will then understand why we consider a balance sheet approach too limited to be of any real use to companies.

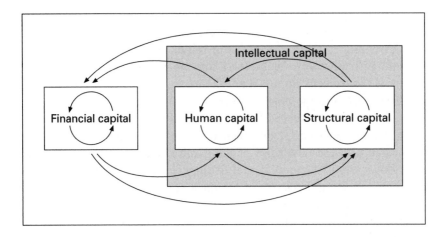

Figure 2.12 The flows of capital

Considering the flows in conjunction with the stocks of intellectual capital adds many dimensions to the problems of assessing it. First of all, intellectual capital flows might include considerable, and variable, time delays. These delays depend on company, industry, country, environmental and situation considerations, so the forecasting of the delays is extremely difficult, if not impossible. Let's take the example of a training course. Once employees get back to work, you would expect them to start applying what they learned straight away. Right? Wrong. Most often, people will need some time to make sense of their teaching, and thus application of the new competencies or skills might be delayed for a while. Also, employees might want to wait for the right occasion to put their new notions into practice, and this occasion might actually occur a long time after the course is over.[43] On the other hand, the increase in competence can generate further learning, both in the people attending the course (as they use their new competencies and build on them) and in other people, as the new competencies spread out through imitation, social encounters and discussions. These time delays might mean that an investment which initially seemed like a waste of money could suddenly become very profitable: the flow merely took its time to create its intended effects. Of course, having 'sleeper' flows wreaks havoc with any accounting or measurement system. How do you decide which flows are going to turn into actual increases in IC, and which ones instead are going to fizzle out?

Which leads us to our next major consideration: intellectual capital is not a zero-sum game. Enormous financial investments to install new IT systems might vanish if the IT systems are not appropriate or company culture discourages their use. Training might absorb huge quantities of funds and fail miserably to convert into an appreciable asset for the company if the trainees do not share the experience or do not even learn in the first place. On the positive side, a small investment in advertising might turn into a very successful slogan and enjoy unforeseen visibility, as Nike discovered when it launched the 'Just Do It' ad campaign. The consequence of these new rules of the game is that only financial flows (that is flows from financial capital to financial capital) need to add up. This, of course, invalidates one of the most powerful tests of accuracy of traditional accounting: balancing.

Finally, there is a question of units of measurement. Financial stocks are all measured in the national unit of currency. IC stocks do not enjoy this uniformity and instead use pure numbers, hours, currency, anything that can help the company get a proxy of the stock in question. So, how do you monitor a flow going from human capital (measured, say, as level of education) into structural capital (measured as hours devoted to the creation of process manuals)? In the example above, we can say intuitively that a receptionist writing a process manual on computer operations does not add to structural capital in the same way that a technical expert in the field hired by the company can. But how do you get the flow report and the stocks report to reflect that?

Thus we have three problems that still need to be solved: we can call them the time-delay, the zero-plus-sum game and the unit of measurement problems. We will tackle some of them in Chapter 5, when our journey will be advanced enough to allow us to find tentative solutions to one of them at least. For the moment, we will have to leave them at the back of our minds and remember them as we progress.

Table 2.1 shows examples of flows from any one form of capital to any other. We believe it is pointless to examine each and every one of them, first of all because we would not add much more than just some explanation of the examples, and second because it would be just another long list.

Table 2.1 Flows of intellectual capital

	Competence value	Attitude value	Intellectual agility value	Relationship value	Organisational value	Renewal and development value	Financial value
Competence value	Reflection on events and theories, conversations, training programmes	Drive to learn, learning environment, conversations	Research and development, cross-fertilisation	Exchange of ideas and skills, reflection on assumptions	Encouragement of learning and reflections (v. 'You are not paid to think')	Research and development, training	Training, hiring of key people
Attitude value	Maturing, shock revelations, confidence boosts	Reinforcement	New behavioural code learning	External examples of attitudes, goodwill towards the company	Culture, tales and legends as means of showing the desired attitude	New requested behaviour	No direct flow
Intellectual agility value	Multiplication of stimuli available	Drive to innovate	Sharpening of intellectual agility through use habit	Increase in stimuli	Team spirit; watch out for conformist and yes cultures	New ways to innovate, adapt, package and imitate	Availability of opportunities to see different solutions
Relationship value	Assessment of quality of partners, contribution to the relations	Fit of the partnership, goal setting for the partnership	New ways to link with partners, choice of new partners	Word-of-mouth, halo effects	Outside orientation (vs. inside)	New relations	Number of relations the company can manage, 'quality' of those relations
Organisational value	Creation of new structures and new solutions	Management by example, corporate legends	Innovation of structure, culture and systems	New organisational forms (virtual organisations)	Only through human contribution	New structures, processes and culture	Availability of alternative solutions, creation of 'cultural' events
Renewal and development value	New directions of discovery and exploration, and expansion, increased attractiveness as business partner	Drive to renew	Creativity and innovation	Suggestion of new alternatives	Cultural orientation towards the future, encouragement of free flow of information	New renewal	Investments in the future development of the company
Financial value	Added value in product and services, consulting	Indirect creation: through other forms of capital	Patent development, cost savings through new solutions	Customer satisfaction, improvement of sales influence, easy access to financing, cost savings	Re-engineering, cost savings	New products	Traditional accounting/financial flows

New Language, New Measures

We thus come to the end of our rather long overview of the forms and flows of intellectual capital. Figure 2.13 shows the complete IC distinction tree, and Table 2.1 summarises the flows. What was the point? Has it really been useful to distinguish all these different stocks of intellectual capital and consider the different flows, or have we just finished an academic hair-splitting exercise?

While you might not have enjoyed this chapter too much, we still believe it was essential to explain exactly what we mean by intellectual capital, what is in it and what is not. If our final purpose is to create an IC measurement system, it is essential to know each form of the data we are going to measure. Such an extensive classification also has the advantage of establishing a common language for all the people involved in the process, thus enabling communication and information sharing. Without such a platform to build on, any conversation will turn into a collection of monologues.

The IC distinction tree, however, is also a prime tool to enable readers to develop knowledge about intellectual capital itself. Although it is fairly straightforward and simple, it is also very comprehensive. It is our hope that following its logic from the highest grouping to the smallest distinction might help readers to understand the issue of intellectual capital as much as it has helped us to focus our research.

Finally, we have repeatedly mentioned in the chapter that using the intellectual capital categories can help the company understand some unclear issues. The value of an employee, for example, and the reaction the financial markets have to the fact that employees leave, can be explained by the comparison financial analysts made between the contribution of the employee (his or her human capital) and his or her remuneration (that is the financial capital he or she was absorbing). Connections and flows between different stocks can become clearer as well. The relationship between the leader's behaviour, the company's motivation and individual motivations, for example, becomes clearer when viewed as a flow of human capital into structural capital and back to human capital, albeit belonging to a different person. Some flows that were not apparent at first have been highlighted: the role of competence in the renewal of relationship capital, for example.

This is not to say that now all the intellectual capital landscape is clearly mapped and in front of us, it is ready for our taking. The role of some forms of capital is still shady and unclear. How does attitude enter into the new intellectual agility capital creation process, for example? Still, the intellectual capital distinction tree, coupled with the flows,

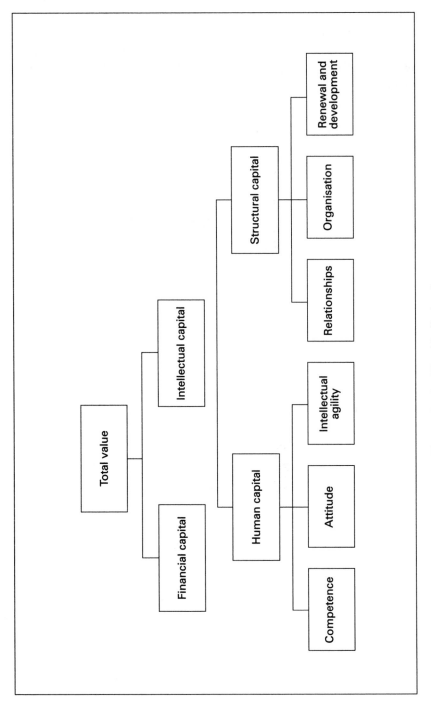

Figure 2.13 The IC distinction tree

represents a good way of understanding what intellectual capital is all about. It is a also a first step in the choice of indicators: it is impossible to choose indicators until what is supposed to be measured is clearly defined. The management task, now, is to select the areas of IC that are most relevant to the company. We will devote the next chapter to the issue of selection.

3 Developing an Intellectual Capital System: the Process Model

COSA, the Caterpillar business unit responsible for most of Europe, the Middle-East, Africa and the CIS (Commonwealth of Independent States – the former USSR), is doing business with clear financial objectives. Its vital performance dimensions are sales growth, keeping the leading market position, and a good return to its owners, Caterpillar Inc. The chief performance measure in COSA is Return-on-Assets (ROA).

Although these three dimensions are absolutely critical, Vito Baumgartner, the chairman of COSA, has been the first to realise that they must be complemented to portray the real value creation throughout the company. Consider the huge investments made in developing the managerial skills of middle-managers in the plants in Belgium and France, as well as in the marketing organisation in Geneva through the COSA Business Academy, a learning partnership with the business school IMD in Lausanne. The value and value-creating potential of this investment show up only indirectly in the financial results. Of course, the one place they do show up is on the income statement – as a cost. The same goes for the substantial investments made in nurturing the already strong ties with numerous and vital Caterpillar dealers throughout its vast geographical area.

As in so many other companies, the top management team of COSA realises that it does not make much sense to have clear financial objectives, with specific levels of ROA to be reached, and then talk only generally about improvement of quality, people as the company's greatest asset, customer satisfaction and so on. If no hard measure is presented to accompany all this talk, all the non-financial objectives will remain too vague and it will be hard for employees on all levels to take them seriously. As a consequence of this vagueness, in the event of a crisis, the company's focus would typically be in restoring profitability as measured by the ROA, and the other targets would take a back seat.

This is why COSA top management has set about creating a new measurement system, which is designed to complement the existing financial one and supply management with necessary information to guide the company towards its goals. This new measurement system would ideally include all the non-financial measures the company was already monitoring, plus some new ones which would be developed as the need arose. They quickly identified a problem, and quite a big one at that: they needed some principles to guide the development of the IC system.

This challenge is not uncommon. Measurement of non-financial data is still more an art than a science, and there are precious few milestones to guide the way in the process of selecting the indicators. Why, might you ask, do we have to select indicators? Actually, indicator selection is nothing new in the business world. Companies have been doing that for a long time in the financial measurement area. However, the business community has maintained the illusion that, as all the measurements were expressed in currency terms, it was child's play to switch from the chosen set of measures to any other set. We all know that things are not that simple, and that what is easy in theory becomes extremely complicated in practice. The incredible number of items that can be classified in two or more different groups make each financial system a world of its own, and translation between two different systems close to impossible. The valuation of stocks, for example, can fluctuate wildly according to management's choice of evaluation method. Thus, a selection is made even among financial indicators, even though often few people are aware of the fact.

The situation becomes more complex in the intellectual capital field. Here, the choice of indicators actually affects the results drastically. If 'number of employees' is chosen as a measure of human capital, no simple transformation can give even a rough idea of 'IT literacy', another measure of the value-creating potential of people. Thus, if transformations were difficult between financial indicators, they are nearly impossible among different intellectual capital indicators. This is why the process of choosing the indicators must be handled with care, lest the wrong data is measured and the company ends up with a worthless (but often expensive) IC measurement system.

In this chapter, we will therefore suggest a model, called the intellectual capital process model, whose purpose is to help companies in this delicate task of selection. We will follow three examples throughout the chapter: Mec-Track, a business unit of COSA, whose story we have already started to examine; SkandiaLink, a unit of Skandia; and a battery manufacturer, which we will call Battery Ltd. This last is a company we have encountered in our research which would prefer to remain anonymous.

Starting from the Business

Let's go back to the COSA story and examine how they solved the starting point problem. Having identified intellectual capital as a strategic issue and initiated a project group including senior top-managers to develop an IC system, they selected a pilot unit inside the company. The choice fell on Mec-Track, an Italian subsidiary of COSA operating in the industry of manufacturing undercarriage components. The main worry, though, was that the new IC system would be so far removed from the everyday reality of the company operations that nobody would care about it, much less monitor the data carefully and try to draw some insights for future directions of the company. As Charles Gustafson, project leader and member of the top-management team of COSA put it: '[We needed] something everybody could sink their teeth into, thus we started with the business'.[1] In practical terms, they decided that the best place to start would be at the heart of the company's identity: the mission.

Mec-Track at the time had just finished a strategic rethinking of its mission. This was actually a fortunate coincidence, because it made managers and employees very receptive to the possible transformation of the mission into practical and observable terms. This is the mission statement of Mec-Track:

To strengthen our worldwide leadership position in the production of undercarriage components by offering to our customers differentiated products of recognised superior value. This mission requires us to:

- create and maintain a work atmosphere favorable to personal growth;
- utilize technologies which are respectful of both the people and the environment;
- confirm the confidence of our shareholders with a sound profitability growth, obtained through the continuous improvement of our management and the development of new business opportunities;
- develop a dynamic and profitable partnership with our customers, suppliers and employees, inspiring excellence, harmony and performance.

The Process Model

So, where does the selection process start? Easy: from ourselves. We have shown this in the story above, and we are going to repeat this over and over again in this chapter: an IC system is good only if it is grounded in the company's identity and strategy. 'Start with the business' has to become the slogan and the standard in the creation of IC measures. In particular, the business concept should be considered: the concept itself can be the vision or the mission of the company, or even the long-term strategy. It has to be something that defines the company's nature and its role in the environment.

As we all know, these statements or documents should define where the company is trying to get, creating some kind of vision of the company's role in the future. Often, though, these mission statements are left hanging in the air and are almost forgotten by everybody in the company. The focus of the company is meeting the short-term objectives (often expressed in financial terms), and no time is left to consider the bigger picture. This attitude causes employees in the company to feel they are fighting fires and not spending time on fire prevention.

An IC system can help companies get past this situation. First of all it translates the company's mission into more quantifiable terms, thus allowing everybody to 'touch' what the company wants to become. Also, it makes trade-offs and connections between different factors and goals much more apparent. Now, in a crisis, management knows that concentrating their attention on financial measures is bound to improve financial performance, At the same time, though, they risk that this focus on one side of the results will cause the deterioration of all the other indicators: if success is measured as achievements across a wide range of indicators, then concentrating on financial results and forgetting about the rest is not a viable option anymore.

To recap, the first step is understanding who you are, and who you want to be. The development of an IC system can be a good occasion to rethink the company's mission, but this is not a required step. The mission statement might very well be the traditional one which the company has been using since its inception, or at least in the recent past.

Once the company has clear ideas on its identity and its long-term goal, it should use these goals as guidelines to identify key success factors. These in turn should become indicators. The information coming from the single measures should then be assembled into different IC categories (Figure 3.1). We will examine the other phases later in the chapter. For now, let's concentrate on the starting point: the business concept.

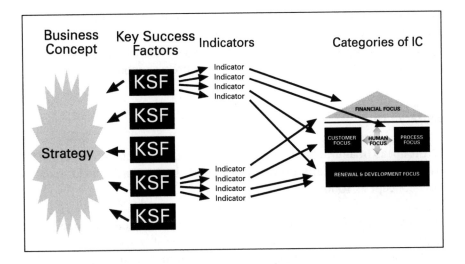

Figure 3.1   The process model (we have used the Skandia model as an example of IC categories)

SkandiaLink

In 1990, new regulations in Sweden allowed for unit-linked life assurance operations. Skandia decided to take advantage of this new business opportunity and created SkandiaLink, first as a part of Skandia Norden, and then, from 1996, as part of the Assurance and Financial Services (AFS) group. SkandiaLink was one of the first units inside the company to follow the pioneering work of the AFS division, and had already developed IC indicators in 1995.

SkandiaLink's mission is: 'to be the marketplace for the movement of selected investment funds and optional insurance'. This mission had been established for quite some time before it was reviewed by SkandiaLink's senior management during the creation of an IC system.

The differences between SkandiaLink's and Mec-Track's concepts are apparent. While Mec-Track's business concept is well rounded and precise, going as far as to identify five areas of concern for the realisation of the mission, SkandiaLink's is more general, giving only the general role the company wants to fulfil in the business world. This, however, does not matter much in the present context. The purpose of the business concept here is to give an idea of what the company thinks of itself and where it wants to go. Both statements achieve this objective and so are as good as any from our point of view. Therefore, there is no special requirement that the business concept has to meet in order to be of any use in the development of IC measures. As long as the concept can create an identity for the company and provide long-term objectives, as any good mission statement should, it can fulfil its role in the process model.

Battery Ltd

A European manufacturer, Battery Ltd produces electrical batteries for use in larger electrically powered machines. Battery articulated its business concept as follows:

- to be perceived as *the* company in the competitive environment
- to achieve high product quality
- to supply modularised products allowing a high degree of customisation
- to achieve a 20 per cent market share
- to maintain a high profitability.

This time, then, it is plain to see that the business concept is expressed in bullet point format as opposed to in a single statement. Once again, as we remarked above, this really has no implication whatsoever on the final result. As long as the concept defines the company and sets it apart from its competitors, then it is good.

This business concept in particular combines elements of direction/mission (to be perceived as the company), goals (market share), generic strategy (the company seems to opt for a 'high perceived value' strategy). All the same, this is not particularly important: the managers of the company came up with that, and that is what they are trying to do and achieve. As a starting point for the IC system, that is all we are looking for.

Outline the Drivers of Future Earnings

The next step is to convert this business concept into some activities that are more specific, and then to identify the correct indicators that capture these activities. Battery, for example, identified eight different main activities that are central to the realisation of strategy:

- production capacity and component deliveries from subsuppliers
- minimisation of activities not in line with the strategy

- choice of co-operation partners
- use of key people and key resources
- capital
- quality control
- internal operating structure
- product development.

The factors are listed in the same order in which they were articulated, which might indicate some kind of higher cognitive centrality for the first ones. While these factors gave the company a clearer idea of where to look for important information on the progress towards the objectives, the company still needed to find appropriate indicators that fitted its operations and its profile. Thus, Battery identified different indicators for each of the eight key factors. Each key factor generated from two to five indicators, giving a total of 28 indicators in all.

Let's take one key success factor and examine it in detail. The use of key people and key resources, for example, yielded five separate indicators. These were:

- personnel turnover
- training budget as a percentage of turnover
- percentage of employees rotating in from or out to cooperation partners
- capacity utilisation
- R&D budget.

Key success factors and their indicators

The second step of the process model, as we have just seen, is translating the business concept into key success factors. Once again, we are not introducing any new concept here. Key success factors have been a cornerstone of strategic theory for a long time. However, we are trying to see these established concepts (the mission before, the factors now) in a new light: this new light will enable us to achieve the creation of totally new measurements for the intellectual capital of the company.

Key success factors (KSFs) indicate, as their name implies, the vital criteria that the particular strategy must meet in order to succeed. The strategy of ensuring low delivered costs throughout the business system, for instance, has a whole different set of success factors than the strategy of achieving high perceived value from the customer's perspective. The latter would allow a price premium whereas the former would mean competing on price. The KSFs are once again a reminder for all strategy makers of what are the factors that need a constant monitoring. There is no limit to the number of key factors a company can identify. If the company enumerates too many criteria, however, then it could be a good idea to prioritise them and concentrate only on the most important ones. Having too many factors to concentrate on would otherwise dilute the focusing effect that should be the prime directive of KSFs. Parsimony should be the guiding light in this work.

The identification of KSFs should be a strategic process of the highest importance. As such, it should originate from the discussions of senior managers, taking their cues from the mission. All the same, the process should not be limited to two or three senior managers. Diversity of opinion and difference of background and experience is fundamental in this instance. Limiting the strategic group too much, or maximising the internal homogeneity of the group might cause group-thinking effects, which can destroy the usefulness of the whole process. Naturally enough, the group cannot be too large either, or the debate on the choice of KSF might drag on forever, due to the inability to reach a clear consensus on the matter.

Up to now, the process model has not really asked for anything out of the ordinary. Both the creation of a mission statement and the determination of key success factors are established practices in the academic and practitioner communities. The third step, however, implies venturing away from the trodden path, and trying to do something new. We are not doing anything strange, however, we are just taking the next logical step forward. Not many companies, all the same, take this step. What we suggest next is to take the key success factors identified in the previous step, and try to understand what are the best indicators that reflect those key success factors.

Basically, then, we are trying to force companies to push their causal effort in identifying the reasons for their result one step further on. Most companies do not do this: they do not measure their level of achievement in some of their key success factors! In a way, it is the same as the oft-repeated homily: 'People are our greatest asset.' That may well be true, but until actions are taken, or measures developed to demonstrate it, these are only empty words. The same goes for key success factors: until a company demonstrates that those really ARE the success factors, they are nothing more than ink on paper. The best way to demonstrate it is actually to measure the company's success in each of the KSFs. Charles Gustafson of Caterpillar notes:

It becomes self-evident. [...] You just go to the people working in the business units and say: 'So, you say that this is important for your business? OK. Do you have a measurement for this?' 'Well, no.' 'Do you think you need a measurement for this?' 'Well, yes: I am the one who said it is important!'

Creating an IC system, then, does not mean inventing new ways to reach success. It just means finally putting into practice what we have been just saying up to now. The quote also highlights another feature of the process model. The people who suggest the mission and the key success factors are the managers of the business units, that is the people who will actually also carry out the measurement. Since they are the ones to select the KSFs, they are more than likely to understand the logic behind the rest of the model, that is putting the KSFs into practice. Thus support is not too difficult to gain, once the first inertia reaction is overcome.

All the same, the creation of an intellectual capital measurement system remains a top-down process. The initial start of the idea, as well as the initial framework, must come from the topmost layers of the organisation. The COSA team had the support of Vito Baumgartner, its chairman, and Don Fites, CEO and Chairman of Caterpillar Inc. in the global headquarters in Peoria, Illinois. The Skandia effort was championed by Jan Carendi, the Director of Skandia AFS, and supported by the President and CEO of the whole company, Björn Wolrath. Top management, though, can supply only the language and the framework – the IC-categories. The filling of the framework, the really juicy part, can be created only at a local level, by the people that know the reality of the business because they are immersed in it every day, 250 days a year.

The added familiarity with the business operations is an absolute requirement. Key success factors are quite general, and in most cases refer to most companies. Take Battery's, which we outlined above. Certainly, those KSFs hold particular importance to Battery and its situation, but which company's success does not depend on the choice of cooperation partners, competent people and quality control? We are not diminishing the importance of the KSF identification step, but KSFs are necessarily general, and thus applicable to more than one company, if not to entire segments or industries. The choice of indicators, on the other hand, reflects the characteristics of the company more closely: in other words, it is more specific.

Mec-Track

The mission statement we quoted above already identified four key areas of interest for Mec-Track's strategy-makers. However, managers decided to draw out the key success factors in higher detail and ultimately fleshed out 53 of them.

Realising that controlling 53 different factors was too ambitious, they tried to prioritise. The prioritisation process was sometimes easy, and sometimes quite difficult. Charles Gustafson recalls:

> Discussing with Mec-Track people, it became clear that if they had a supplier who had been a supplier for five years, all these other things [all the other factors] would already happen.

Thus, supplier relations, an issue in the mission statement, could be controlled and measured by the length of the relationship. Other issues were not so quickly translated into KSFs or indicators, and getting to a manageable list was a long iterative process, as it often is.[2] In Mec-Track's case, the process was actually performed by two people only, the head of the organisation and the accounting manager. This, of course, enabled them to proceed rapidly through what could have become a long selection process.

Mec-Track, as we can see, had a very detailed process, much more so than SkandiaLink. A possible reason might be found in the fact that, while SkandiaLink is an 'old hand' at IC systems (having already had three years of experience now), Mec-Track's experiment is a first attempt. It is therefore understandable that one company would try to examine all possible options, while the other would quickly limit the discussion to the more interesting ones.

Having cut down its list of KSFs to 26, Mec-Track proceeded to select the appropriate indicators for each of them. Of course, having so many KSFs, the level of detail in each of them was so specific that often the choice was self-apparent. For example, having ascertained that longevity of relationship was a key KSF for establishing a good relationship with a supplier, it is obvious that the indicator for that KSF would be the number of years of association.

For all KSFs, however, appropriate measurements are chosen, It is important to stress that, in some cases, or actually we should say in most cases, one KSF required several measurements. The difficulty in measuring intangibles means, of course, that all indicators used are proxies for the KSFs. Sometimes the proxies are right on the mark (for instance the longevity of relationship/years of relationship (example given above), but in other cases more than one proxy measure may be needed to get a clear and correct picture.

We will now concentrate on one of the four key areas we mentioned above in Mec-Track's mission statement, and examine the KSFs developed for it. Let's take the third bullet point, the profitability growth obtained through continuous improvement and the development of new business opportunities. According to Mec-Track management, to achieve this goal the key success factors are: new products and/or new customers, make/buy reviews, increase customer penetration, financial management, manufacturing process review, commercial process review, lower period costs, benchmarking, hiring/selection, permanent/ temporary employment, usage of innovative techniques, quality. After prioritisation, it was decided to focus on:

- new products and/or new internal/external customers
- increase customer penetration
- manufacturing process reviews
- commercial process reviews
- hiring/selection
- permanent/temporary employment
- usage of innovative techniques
- quality.

Table 3.1 shows the key success factors we have examined, and their corresponding indicators.

Table 3.1   Measures for Mec-Track

Key success factors	Indicators
New products and/or new internal/external customers	- Number of new products - Number of new customers - Success ratio
Increase customer penetration	- Percentage of customer business
Manufacturing process reviews	- Productivity index - Number of processes reviewed - Number of processes changed
Commercial process reviews	- Productivity index - Number of processes reviewed - Number of processes changed
Hiring/selection	- Percentage rated acceptable at first review

Table 3.1 (cont'd)

Key success factors	Indicators
Permanent/temporary employment	■ Ratio of temporary/total employment
Usage of innovative techniques	■ Number of patents filed ■ Number of ideas implemented from the suggestion box
Quality	■ Traditional indicators ■ ISO and customer certification

ScandiaLink

ScandiaLink senior managers identified five separate key success factors for the company:

■ To establish long-term relationships with satisfied customers. This in turn implies having profitable customers, because any satisfied customer of a financial company is prone to come back with additional requests for services in time.

■ To establish long-term relationships with parties in the distribution channels. Although supplier relations have been recognised as a key areas by many companies, the topic is particularly important for SkandiaLink and Skandia in general, because they have chosen to dispense with the proprietary distribution networks, and instead use existing banks to commercialise their products. In this situation it is obvious that the power of retailers is quite high, so it is in the interests of the company to keep them very happy.

■ To implement efficient administrative routines. Assurance companies are almost the stereotype of bureaucracy, but Skandia prides itself in its ability to cut the red tape to a minimum.

■ To create an IT system capable of supporting operations. This KSF actually ties in with the previous one. However, SkandiaLink decided to separate the two to highlight the importance they assign to IT systems.

■ To employ satisfied and competent employees. It might seem strange to have competence and satisfaction in the same sentence, as they are not conventionally correlated. Skandia, however, believes that competent employees are better equipped to respond to the challenge of their work, and are thus more satisfied with themselves and their jobs.

Although a relatively small number of KSFs were highlighted by the company, each factor then generated many different indicators. In the end, 24 indicators were selected for tracking in 1997. Some of the indicators actually referred to more than one KSF. This is natural and understandable. Because the KSFs are related to each other (for example, efficient administration increases customer satisfaction), it is obvious that some of the indicators should apply to more than one success factor.

In particular, let's examine the satisfied customer success factor. To assess and improve customer satisfaction, SkandiaLink management chose the following indicators:

- satisfied customer index
- customer barometer
- new sales
- market share
- lapse rate
- average response time at the call centre
- discontinued calls at the call centre
- average handling time for completed cases
- number of new products.

Putting It Together

As we mentioned before, SkandiaLink presented 24 separate indicators in its final IC measurement system. Each indicator, however, told only part of the story, and was thus meaningless taken on its own. Moreover, the indicators needed to be expressed in term of forms of capital identified by the company, to create a common language between the theoretical thoughts behind the IC model and the practical indicators.

SkandiaLink thus decided to use the work done previously by the Skandia Assurance and Financial Service unit, summarised by the Navigator.[4] The five areas selected to group the indicators cover financial capital and the first level distinction of intellectual capital, human and structural capital. Structural capital is already subdivided into its three different components: process capital (which we called organisational capital), customer capital (for us, relationship capital), and renewal and development capital.

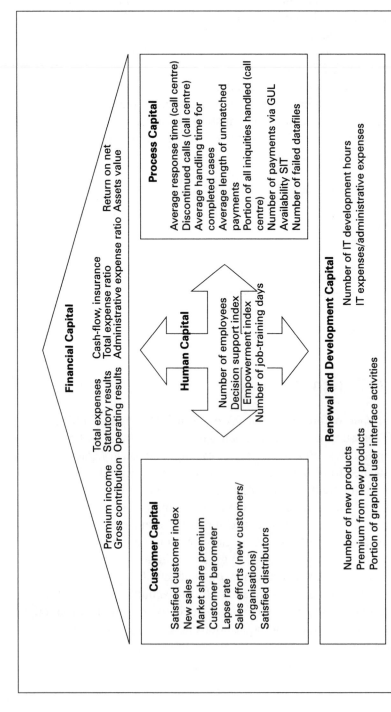

Figure 3.2 The SkandiaLink Navigator

Indicators derived from each of the five KSFs we mentioned above were thus categorised in these five focus areas (Figure 3.2). It is interesting to note that indicators derived from one KSF do not necessarily end up in the same focus area. For example, indicators chosen to monitor the improvement of customer satisfaction can be found in the customer focus (the satisfied customer index, the customer barometer, the amount of new sales, market share, lapse rate), the process focus (average response time at the call centre, discontinued calls at the call centre, average handling time for completed cases) and renewal and development focus (new products).

Mec-Track

Caterpillar uses a similar but slightly different model to group indicators and improve the focus. They call it the IC Base, and it considers four aspects of intellectual capital, as well as three aspects of financial capital (Figure 3.3). The similarities between Skandia's model and Mec-Track's are evident, as summarised in Table 3.2, which also includes comparisons with the model used by Battery, which we will examine below.

Table 3.2 Different names for similar focus areas

Skandia	Caterpillar	Battery
Human Focus	People	Human Capital
Process Focus	Process	Business Process Capital
Customer Focus	Relationship	Customer and Relationship Capital
Renewal and Development Focus	Innovation	Renewal and Development Capital

We have already remarked on the fact that Mec-Track's KSFs were very precise. This precision meant that each KSF generated indicators for a single focus area, unlike the situation in SkandiaLink. Thus, in Mec-Track's case all indicators coming from any given KSF ended up in just one focus area. The grouping of indicators became a grouping of KSFs. This, however, is an exception to the rule.

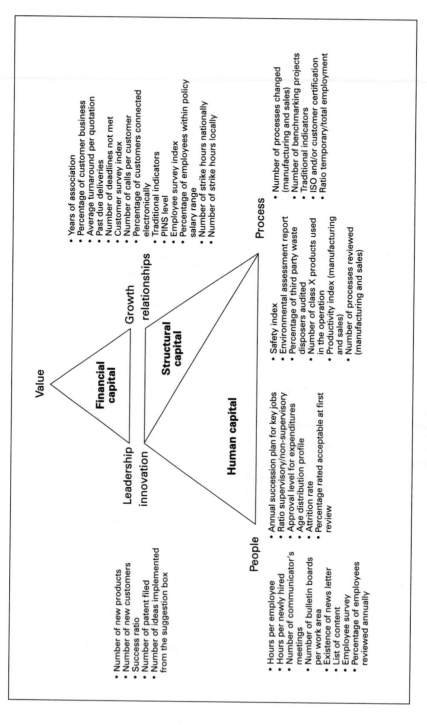

Figure 3.3   Mec-Track's IC Base

Battery

Battery used a model supplied by the venture capitalist to put together its own IC system. The model identified four different IC focuses, as shown in Figure 3.4. Table 3.2 shows the comparison between the forms of capital identified in this instance and those used by Skandia and us. As in the case of SkandiaLink above, indicators originating from one single key success factor ended up in different categories.

The Next Step

If you have managed to get this far, you should have cleared your ideas on how to create an IC system. The beauty of it, but, from another perspective, also the sadness of it, is that such a system is never perfected. Increased use will reveal faults, and new work will be required to correct these faults and to improve the choice of indicators. Practice will show how to sharpen the focus of the image that this system is conveying to management.

During the first attempt, most companies tend to use non-financial indicators that are already present in the existing measurement system: customer satisfaction, market share, defect rate, and so on. This is absolutely normal, and indeed commendable. We have already said this and we will never get tired of repeating it: the real added value of an IC system is the new perspective it gives to the company. Intellectual capital is there even before the IC system is in place, and it is true that some parts of it are already being measured in the common practice of the business world. There is therefore nothing wrong in trying to become familiar with the new framework through familiarity with the contents. Even using the old indicators, the IC system might be able to lend some new insights through new combinations of indicators that will highlight aspects of the company's intellectual capital which nobody thought about before.

This initial use of existing indicators must not constrain the company, though. There has to be freedom on one hand and readiness on the other to change some or all the indicators in the IC system to suit the increased understanding of the problem that comes with experience. Some indicators will be slightly changed, some added, and some discarded altogether. Some indicators might even be moved from one category to another, because managers have realised that their real information content lies in a different direction than previously thought.

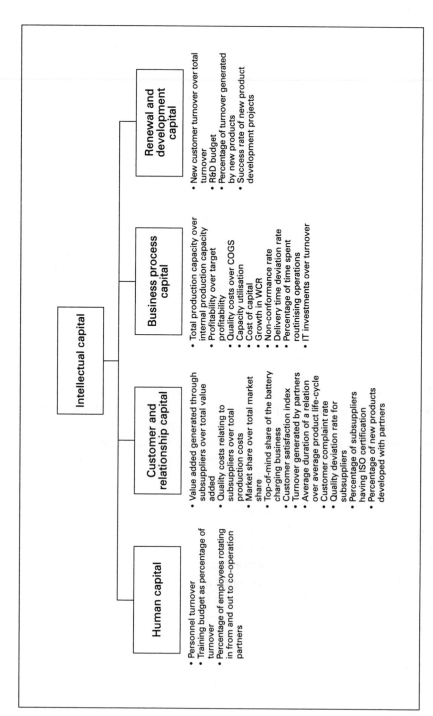

Figure 3.4 Battery's Intellectual Capital System

A brief note must also be made on another, related subject. As we stated at the beginning of the chapter, and then went on to demonstrate during the chapter as a whole, the IC system is rooted in the strategy. Strategy, as we all know, is an annual exercise. Should the IC system therefore change completely from one year to the next? This is against the established accounting practice.

The solution is actually quite simple. The IC system is rooted in strategy, yes, but in the long-term strategy expressed by the mission statement, not in the year-on-year strategy. True, some of the indicators might change due to changes in strategic direction, or even achievement of goals, but these kinds of change are slow and almost imperceptible. Strategy will be determined by the IC system, and will determine for itself the relative importance of the different focus areas. As Robert Nilsson, IC controller for SkandiaLink, stated:

> Between 1996 and 1997, the focus in the SkandiaLink's Navigator has shifted from the process focus to the customer focus, even though it does not show.

The indicators in the two Navigators are very similar, if not the same. Thus, though it might be possible that an IC system from one year is totally different to that from the previous year, it is highly unlikely.

Both Caterpillar and Skandia are also trying to scale their models. COSA is trying to apply it to companies higher up in the hierarchy of the group. The attempt right now is to develop a model for every company inside COSA, and for the whole company as such.

Skandia, on the other hand is trying to scale down the model, to arrive at a Navigator on a personal level. Thus, the Navigator that one level prepares is handed down to the level below as a framework for its activities. The lower level then gets some objectives from the Navigator, but has to express these objectives in terms of a new Navigator applying to this new level. This way, all employees in the company actually see what their contribution is to the general goals of the company; each one is involved in the process model (although at different levels) and everybody understands the concept of intellectual capital. Lower level navigators are less stable, as they tend to concentrate on shorter-term activities. Their trend, therefore, is to change every year quite radically, reflecting the fact that last year's objectives have been reached and the company has to move on.

The greatest use of a complete IC system, however, is its potential to help the company monitor the dynamics of its IC, and thus manage its value more accurately. We will devote the next two chapters to these topics.

4 Consolidating Intellectual Capital Measurements: The IC-Index Approach

Using the previous chapters of the book, readers should now be able to develop their own IC management system, similar to the ones we have seen for COSA, SkandiaLink and Battery. Once the system is in place, however, its limitations will become apparent.

Remember that intellectual capital is by definition intangible and that the only possible measurements are proxy variables, or indicators. These indicators will be expressed in the most diverse units of measurement: pure numbers, number of hours, of workers, of computers, of transactions, of new products, of successful pitches, of solutions suggested on the hot-line, and so on. At first glance, it seems to be a nightmare even to try to assess trade-off between two alternatives. If the number of customers has declined but the remaining customers are more satisfied, for instance, has the company's customer capital increased or decreased? Obviously it depends on the size of the decrease in the number of customers and the amount of the increase in customer satisfaction.

Another basic problem with the IC system as we know it remains the difficulty of carrying out inter-company comparisons. In fact such comparisons will be possible only if two companies, or units, have selected the same measurement (similar forms of, and flows among) for their intellectual capital. Companies serving the same customer segment are likely to identify similar indicators, at least in part. For instance, insurance companies might be interested in the number of contracts per employee, speed of response to claims and number of policy renewals of the policies, while consumer-product manufacturers will be more interested in cycle time, quality of supplies, and brand image. Thus, comparisons inside homogeneous groups can be made, although with some difficulty, because at least some if not most of the measures will be common. The more distant two companies are in their activities, however, the less comparison will be possible, as they will probably focus on totally different indicators to represent their intellectual capital performance.

Firms operating in two totally different industries will have very few measures in common, and thus comparisons seem meaningless. In this case, the two companies might share only the generic measures, and maybe not even all of them. This inability to make comparisons across industries will be especially troublesome for investors, who can choose among companies operating in totally different markets and industries. The current effort within the financial community to make comparisons between companies highlights the need for new, comparable IC measures.

The list of weak spots of an IC system is still not complete. Obviously, the creation of intellectual capital should not be pursued at any cost. To create intellectual capital, financial capital has to be consumed. It is important to understand what the return on investments of financial capital and intellectual capital are in terms of shareholder value increase or decline. What is needed is a measure of IC efficiency, something that can be related it to the more traditional financial efficiency measures. Otherwise, the risk is that intellectual capital practices and reporting will just be the next management fad that some people accuse it to be. If such efficiency measures can be introduced and used, IC practices will produce insights that inevitably will be on top of the managerial agenda for companies entering the twenty-first century.

This lack of efficiency measures ties in with another weak spot, that is the lack of relations between IC and the financial and physical side of the company. We already stated that intellectual capital is not a zero-sum game, and thus flows of financial capital can turn in little or no increase in IC, and vice versa. There is an evident need, then, to understand the relationship between the two, to be able to improve the 'transformation efficiency', that is the efficiency of the company in transforming IC into financial value and financial capital into intellectual capital.

All of these factors are pushing the intellectual capital theory and practice towards the development of what Johan Roos and Göran Roos labelled the 'second generation' of IC practices.[1] Whereas the first generation is all that has been discussed in this book so far, the second generation consolidates all the different measurements into a single index (or at least a small number of indices), and then relates this index to shareholder value.

This development is the next logical step in the practice of intellectual capital management. In particular, second generation practices move in two directions:

▨ They consolidate all the different measures for intellectual capital
  into one single measure.
▨ They correlate the changes in intellectual capital with the changes in
  market (and thus shareholder) value.[2]

Both directions obviously aim at the same goal that motivated the
creation of first generation practices: the improvement of the visualisation
of the value-creating processes of the company so that they can be
managed comprehensively. In particular, the consolidation of the indicators into a few aggregated indices in effect creates a bottom line for intellectual capital, a synthesis measure to check all alternatives against. This
synthesis allows managers to evaluate alternative strategies, highlighting
their effect on intellectual capital as a whole. Thus, second generation
practices enable managers to assess the IC situation of a company holistically, whereas the first generation practices give information only on the
single components of intellectual capital.

Obviously, second generation practices do not substitute for first generation ones; rather, they complement them. Running a company with only
aggregated indices is unthinkable: it would be impossible to understand
what caused a given change in the aggregated index without having a
comprehensive system that examined all the components of the aggregation. But managing a company the other way, without aggregated indices,
would be like trying to assess someone's medical condition by examining
their cells one by one.

Similar considerations also apply to the second task of second generation practices: the correlation of IC with shareholder value. This, in a way,
is the culmination of all the work on intellectual capital: the increase in
shareholder value. If IC could not be used for this purpose, then why
bother? Value creation should be the ultimate test of any strategy the
comany is pursuing, and IC is no exception. As Table 1.1 demonstrated,
the correlation between IC and market value is strong indeed, and thus
worth exploring in its own right.

This chapter will examine the consolidation of IC indicators into IC-
indices, while the next and final chapter of this book will consider the
correlation of IC with market value. The creation of a complete set of IC-
indices is followed step by step, starting from a review of the existing
indicators, then moving on to the actual consolidation part. Consequences of such an approach will also be discussed, and the real-life
effects of the adoption of an IC-Index approach will be shown with two
different companies.

Complement Stock Measurements with Flow Measurements

Companies implementing IC practices tend to adopt a balance sheet approach and ignore the dynamic flows between different forms of capital. Because the balance sheet approach to IC, like the Skandia Navigator, provides only a snapshot in time it must be complemented with the information on what has happened between the two photographs, that is the flows of capital.

The problem has already been examined in Chapter 2,[3] but it is worth mentioning it again. Flows of capital thus need to be targeted specifically with some indicators, to create a complete picture of the company's IC situation.

It is not enough, for example, to examine the efficiency of the processes of the company's operations. It is also very important to examine the improvement in these processes, through re-engineering and rethinking, which is a flow from renewal and development value. Also, the impact that these processes have in the creation of new relationships, for example interposing too much red tape for the establishment of a new joint venture, should be assessed: it is, of course, a flow from organisational to relationship value. Even more importantly, do the processes frustrate the employees (a negtive flow towards attitude value)? Or do they allow all people working in the company to exploit their own competencies to the fullest, always challenging them to discover new skills and to study new fields (a positive flow to competence value)?

Flows indicators can thus convey much more information than stocks can alone. Moreover, it is information that captures the dynamic operations of the company, an area that was completely overlooked by the 'balance sheet' approach.

Reviewing IC Indicators

To consolidate IC measurements into a single figure, the first step is to understand what to consolidate. This implies that all the indicators chosen for a IC system should be reviewed and, most probably, be adjusted. Because IC measurement is about proxies there is a need for multiple indicators for each form, or focus area of intellectual capital. This multiplies the data to keep track of, adding to the overall complexity of the measurement system – not a desirable result, but in our case not an uncommon one. In our experience, companies tend to produce long lists of indicators of intellectual capital data. What is often missing is the understanding of the priorities and the relationships between the different measurements. Thus, all indicators are taken to be equally important, and this of course makes the management tasks that much more complex.

Moreover, most measurements used in companies and prescribed by scholars and consultants tend to lack a solid theory justifying their existence and specifying the cause and effect relationship involved. For instance, what is the theory behind measuring the percentage of employees above and below a certain age? This is the case for many of the indicators in the examples mentioned in this and other books on IC. Although this may not be surprising, because the measurements emerge from a bottom-up process relating to key success factors rather than theories, it is not good enough if companies want to move beyond the initial benefits of IC practices discussed so far.

This is why it is necessary to go through the list of indicators, and understand what each one is really aiming to capture, what it actually measures, and what a change in this indicator would signify for the company. At this stage, it is also important to check (once again) for precision, robustness and relevance of each indicator. Often, the use of many indicators (demanded by the fact that we can use only proxies) may blur the picture instead of clearing it up. It is essential that managers are sure that the indicators chosen not only satisfy the statistical criterion of robustness but also express specifically and precisely what the company is looking for.

The review will most likely transform the indicators, and make them seemingly more complex. This complexity, however, can easily be handled by today's spreadsheets, and usually generates a much bigger improvement in precision. Complexity in calculation, therefore, is not a big worry because power computers can handle it.

This review of the indicators should also establish their ranking. Of course, every IC measure is important, otherwise it would not be there at all. All the same, because aggregation is not easy, it is better to select a handful indicators for each IC form and flow. This way, though some information might be lost, complexity is kept in check. It is better to concentrate on a few indicators than to try to keep track of many different ones simultaneously. Every unit or company has to prioritise and select which IC forms and flows and indicators really drive the business (and, as a consequence, profit). Remember that sometimes the indicator conveying the most information is not the most obvious one: who would have thought that the number of trucks leaving the factory, for example, would be a good measurement of profitability? Nonetheless, an example given later in this chapter will show just that.

Once the list of indicators has considerably shrunk, each one must be expressed as a dimensionless number. For some indicators, it will be easy (training can be expressed as number of hours on total working hours, for example), but for some it will be more difficult (number of new patents filed, for example). All the same, mathematical transformations should help the company arrive at a formulation of all its main measurements as dimensionless numbers. In a worst-case scenario, value judgement can be used to place the company inside a scale, in comparison with the closest competitors. These value judgements should be the articulation of tacit and explicit insights into the company and its business.

Building IC-Indices[4]

Armed with a handful of robust indicators for each IC form and IC flow that we feel are important, it is possible to consolidate these into one or several indices. This is not new and many managers tend to do this by 'gut feeling'. Second generation IC practices, therefore, only help managers to articulate this feeling. Articulating it helps the company to bring to the fore the assumptions underlying its dynamics, thus opening them to discussion.

A few years ago, Mr Smith, the founder and owner of a medium-sized company that manufactured sausages, decided to retire from the active management of it. He kept the ownership nonetheless, and regularly participated in meetings with the new top management to review the standing of his investment. The managers were amazed by Mr Smith's knowledge of the company's profitability, which even extended as far as pointing out trends that they had not yet noticed. This happened even though the owner himself seemed to have no active contact with any member of the top management team. Curious, managers started asking if Mr Smith had been coming to the plant and talking to any one at all. It emerged that he walked daily from his house to the plant (a short walk, as the factory was built on family land adjoining the house), and talked to the guard at the main gate.

The guard was summoned and questioned about his conversations with Mr Smith. At first he said that Mr Smith only made small talk but thinking about it further, he realised that there were three questions that Mr Smith was always asking. First, he wanted to know how many employees failed to show up in the morning. He did not care about the causes, he just wanted to know the number. Then, he asked how many trucks of finished products had left the factory that day. Finally, he asked how many trucks of "defective products" (including defective and rejected products) had left the company that day. Because Mr Smith talked with nobody else who had even a vague inkling of what the company was doing, managers concluded that he was actually estimating trends in profitability from those three questions, outguessing the managers who had much more data at their command and the best analysts and computers to correlate the data.

This true story teaches us some lessons that can be applied to intellectual capital practices. It is clearly possible to understand any variable, such as the financial health of the company, by looking at only a handful of indicators. Three or four variables might yield on their own 80 per cent of the useful information, whereas to fill the remaining 20 per cent gap you might need 30 or more indicators. Of course, given the time and ability, it is useful to consider the additional 30 variables. All the same, it is the main three that need to be carefully monitored if the variable in question is to be kept in check. Prioritisation of the different measures in the system, therefore, can help managers deal with the increasing complexity of it.

Sometimes useful management insights can be gained simply from trends; precise measurements may not be necessary, in the spirit of 'it is better to be roughly right than precisely wrong'. Mr Smith did not have precise profitability data, only some rough indicators. Even so, the managers with all the right numbers had missed the trend.

Let's examine another illustration. A few years ago the CEO of an European airline was weighing his options. The VP for Marketing was pushing for a new and improved service for the business traveller segment. This included investments in extra leg space, and fixed tables and power outlets for laptop computers. The idea was to introduce these services on both long-haul and intra-European flights. The VP for Marketing estimated that this move would create high perceived value among business customers, in line with the indications from the latest in-flight survey. The upside of the investment was increased customer satisfaction, increased retention rate and, thus, increased revenue and profits.

At the same time the VP for Operations had put together a plan for a revamp of the maintenance services for the aircraft. With the new programme, aircraft would be able to convey the results of their self-diagnostic routines before arriving at the destination. This meant that the ground service team would be better prepared to service the aircraft and, thus, maintenance time would be reduced. The cost savings potential was considerable.

If that was not enough, the VP for Human Resources had suggested that flight attendants should be trained in more languages, particularly those of Far Eastern and Eastern European countries. This again would aim to increase the satisfaction and loyalty of travellers.

Unfortunately, due to financial constraints all three options could not be implemented at the same time. The CEO felt that all three would have very positive effects and indeed increase profits but he was unsure as to which one to implement first. In this situation, even forecasts with first generation IC practices would not be very helpful. This would tell the CEO simply that customer, process and human capital respectively would increase as financial capital decreased at first, and rose afterwards (in the forecasts). What this CEO really needed was a single, consolidated measure of IC growth and decline, and how this related to financial performance.

Such a measure must summarise all the dynamics of intellectual capital previously discussed. What is needed is the intellectual capital equivalent of the 'trucks out with finished products/trucks out with discarded products/employees in' triad of measures that Mr Smith was using for his sausage company. Although Mr Smith was resorting to three different measures, these were then integrated into one 'gut feeling' measure in his brain.

After the review of their indicators, companies should have a limited list of measurements, all expressed in dimensionless numbers. Now the consolidation can start. The process of consolidation itself is fairly simple. The indicators chosen should be weighted, and then united into a single, summarising index, taking into account the interdependence, causalities and insufficiencies.

Care should be taken when aggregating indices, however. To create an overall corporate IC-Index, only indices on the same level should be aggregated. Structural capital and human capital can be aggregated, whereas human capital and renewal and development value, for instance, should not be aggregated. Renewal and development has first to be aggregated with the other forms of structural capital, and only then with human capital. If some categories are not considered in the calculation of the final index, then effectively they have been assigned a weight of zero, indicating that they do not have an effect on the final stock of intellectual capital. While such a situation is possible, it is highly improbable, given the high aggregation level of the capital forms considered.

The problem of choosing the right indicators and capital forms have already been discussed.[5] Here we will expand a bit on this subject, considering the choice of weights. Three factors should guide the company's choices of indicators: the strategy, the characteristics of the company and the characteristics of the industry the company operates in (Table 4.1).

Table 4.1   The selection of capital forms, weights and indicators

	Selection of capital forms	Selection of weights	Selection of indicators
Strategy			
Business			
Company			

Each factor influences one of the three selection processes the company has to go through. When selecting the important capital forms, strategy is the key issue. As we discussed above, strategy is the guiding light in making sense of different IC forms, and in understanding which ones will help the company to realise its strategic goals. Business characteristics and industry characteristics exercise only an indirect influence, because they influence the strategy itself.

When choosing indicators, the knowledge of the day-to-day operations is essential. That is why Chapter 3 recommended making the choice of indicator a bottom-up process. In the choice of weights, the main consideration in the mind of managers has to be the relative importance each capital form has in the creation of value in the particular business of the company. It is here, therefore, that industry dynamics become extremely important, at the relative expense of the particular strategy a company is pursuing and the characteristics of its operations.

Let's look back at the three companies we examined in the last chapter, and try to imagine how they would rank their indicators in one of their capital forms. SkandiaLink, for example, has chosen the following indicators to measure customer capital:

- customer satisfaction index
- customer barometer
- new sales

- market share
- lapse rate
- number of new customers/organisations
- satisfied distributors.

Given their KSFs, which were examined previously, the most important indicators here would be the retention rate (expressed as 1-lapse rate) and the customer satisfaction index, as both measure the satisfaction of customers, a key focus area for the company. Distributors' satisfaction is probably as important, identifying another key area of SkandiaLink's strategy. The customer barometer comes next in importance, assessing the customer base mix and composition. Then market share, and least important of all, the new sales and the number of new customers. This is not to say that these last three indicators are not important, or that they should be disregarded: given SkandiaLink's strategy, though, to concentrate on long-term customer relations and on satisfied distributors, other factors take precedence. Given this ranking, management could then choose precise weights for each indicator.

Mec-Track identified the following indicators for their innovation focus:

- number of new products
- number of new customers
- success ratio
- number of patents filed
- number of ideas implemented from the suggestion box.

As Mec-Track's strategy was directed towards the growth of profitability through the exploitation of new opportunities, the most important indicator would be the success ratio of new products, followed closely by the number of new products. The number of new customers would be slightly less important, and still less important would be the number of patents filed and the number of ideas implemented from the suggestion box.

Finally, Battery chose these indicators to represent its business process capital:

- total production capacity/internal production capacity
- profitability/target profitability
- quality costs/COGS
- capacity utilisation

- growth in WCR
- non-conformance rate
- delivery time deviation rate
- percentage of time spent routinising operations
- IT investments/turnover.

Again, judging from the KSFs mentioned before in Chapter 3, the most important indicators seem to be the quality costs and the non-conformance rate on one side, and the production capacity and the capacity utilisation on the other. Slightly less important is the percentage of time spent routinising operations (a key activity for the development of the internal structure), and the IT investments. All the other indicators are less central to the company strategy, and thus should get lower weights.

Consequences of an IC-Index Approach

First and foremost, an IC-Index solves the problem that first generation practices had when facing the choice between two or more strategic alternatives. Through the creation of a single index summarizing all intellectual capital, an IC bottom line, if you will, managers are suddenly in a position to make comparisons between alternative strategies, and thus choose the strategy most suited to the goals of the company. Where before they could use only 'gut feeling', managers can now rely on a more reliable tool. The existence of such a tool enables them to put into practice what were formerly just vague notions, and it will also bring the issue of intellectual capital management to the attention of companies who do not use such practices yet.

Let's take for example a US-based financial products company, which we will call Yankee Finance. In the next chapter the example will be considered in detail, but some of the observations are more appropriate here. After using a traditional IC system for a couple of years, Yankee Finance decided to adopt a second generation approach and tried to consolidate its indicators, using as a basis a Skandia-like distinction of the capital forms. Thus, they reviewed and changed some of their indicators, and concentrated on the most important ones, shortening the list of variables considerably. The final list looked something like this:

- Relationship capital index
  - growth in number of relationships
  - growth in trust

- customer retention
- distribution channel productivity and quality
- Human capital index
  - fulfillment of key success factors
  - value creation per employee
  - training efficiency and effectiveness
- Infrastructure capital index
  - efficiency
  - effectiveness
  - key success factor utilisation
  - distribution efficiency
- Innovation capital index
  - ability to generate new business
  - ability to generate good products
  - growth
  - ability to productify.

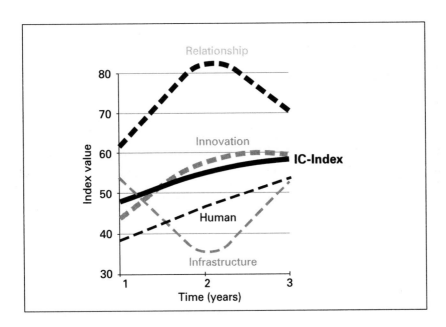

Figure 4.1   Yankee Finance IC-Indices

They then assigned weights to each of the indicators, and plotted the aggregated indices together (Figure 4.1). A trade-off between indices became apparent: relationship and infrastructure index were negatively related. At the first meeting, management tried to understand what had happened. Their conclusion is that in year one they focused very much on customer satisfaction and this, of course, sent efficiency down. This scared shareholders, who pushed for cost-control programmes, which were implemented in year two. They were obviously effective, as evidenced by the increase in efficiency, but customers left because they felt they were not given the same excellent service anymore.

While management knew this before, the graph made it easy to discuss and compare opinions. Moreover, it indicated that a gradual increase in customer satisfaction would have been much more desirable: it would not have caused the efficiency problems, because the organisation would have had time to adjust. Also, it would probably have resulted in higher satisfaction in the end: the lapse rate of customers was mainly caused by a perceived fall in service standard, which would not have happened had the service standard been gradually increased to the present level.

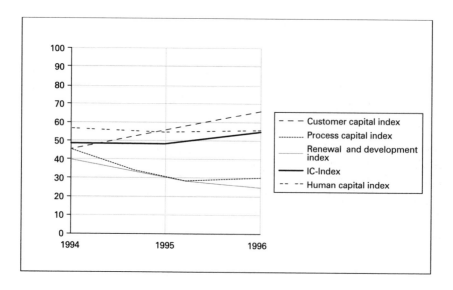

SOURCE: Roos & Roos (1997)

Figure 4.2   Trade-off effects for intellectual capital

Let us illustrate this point with a further example.[6] Two years ago, top management in a manufacturing company wanted to increase dramatically the level of customer satisfaction and retention rate: in our terms, this translates into an increase in customer capital. Figure 4.2 shows their intellectual capital performance, tracking their progress towards their goal through the five indices reflective of the main focus areas of the Skandia Navigator. As the figure shows, the company indeed managed to achieve its goal: the customer capital index increased from 45 in 1994 to 67 in 1996. However, what managers did not consider in their strategy formulation was that this increase could cost more than just financial capital. In fact, what happened was that the process capital index and (to a slightly lesser extent) the renewal and development index both declined during the same time period.

Conversations with the top management team clearly showed that the two different IC dynamics were linked. Managers complained that the strong emphasis on customer capital had made it difficult for employees to focus on improving internal efficiency and keeping up product development at the same time, in a similar dynamic to that seen in Yankee Finance. The final result was positive: in the time period considered, the aggregated IC-Index increased from 43 to 54, reflecting a significantly increased 'hidden value' of the company. But, without the reduction in process capital and renewal & development capital, the growth in IC would have been much higher. Again, managers were now able to pinpoint a problem which before was just a general feeling that there was something wrong.

Thus, the main benefit of an IC-Index is making uncertain and subjective feelings about what is happening in the company more visible, thus forcing management to discuss the issues and come up with a solution. Still, there are other important areas were the contributions of an IC-Index approach are fundamental. For example, comparisons in intellectual capital become possible, and especially in intellectual capital performance. Benchmarks can be established both in absolute terms and in percentage increases. What's more, benchmarks can be established at different levels of aggregation, starting from market segment and industry to the national and transnational.

Finally, an IC-Index visualises a greater part of the company to external stakeholders. In the quest for added clarity, transparency and completeness of outside information, an IC-Index can help the company signify to the market its hidden value creation processes, and thus help the market make a better assessment of the company's value. This can decrease the vulnerability to certain external events: if the financial market is made aware of all the company's capabilities, then it will not discount the company's value so much when an external event is challenging the company's position. Because intellectual capital is the real root of value, the IC-Index can also be useful to analysts in predicting future value trends. More information on these subjects can be found in the next chapter.

Examining Strengths and Weaknesses of an IC-Index

It is important to note that the IC-Index only indirectly measures the stock of intellectual capital a company has, resulting as it does in a dimensionless number. However, it directly measures the changes in the IC stocks, and it does so remarkably well. Thus we have created an index which has some relationship, linear or non-linear, with the actual intellectual capital stock of the company, and therefore can be used to monitor the dynamics of IC. In practice, this means that if the IC-Index increases from 4 to 8, the IC of a company has not necessarily doubled. It has grown, however, and more so than if the new index had been 7 or 7.5. This insight is typically more than enough.

Managers using an IC-Index are finally able to understand the effects a particular strategy has on the IC of a company, and compare two alternatives to understand which one is preferable from an IC point of view. Although is not always necessary to know the absolute value of a variable, the knowledge of the dynamics, that is growth or decline over time, of this variable can be more than enough.

An IC-Index is obviously not an ultimate and all-encompassing measure. But, this measure gives information on the actual stock of intellectual capital. Inter-company comparisons must therefore be limited to the 'intellectual capital performance' of the companies themselves. While this is certainly not the best situation, it still allows for more informed decision in the comparisons of companies than was possible before. Unlike many other performance measures, however, an IC-Index has some memory, that is it takes into account the performance from past periods of time. Thus, one-off special events might have a very strong influence on the index, and shift it to a higher level. This higher level attained will be evident even in the following years.

Some might remark that the IC-Index depends on value judgments, both in the choice of weights and, sometimes, in the assessment of the value of a given indicator. This is true, but all the same this puts it in exactly the same position as regular accounting data. Although many people live in the belief that accounting data is precise because it deals with integer digits, most managers are familiar with the impact that 'favourable' accounting can have on the company situation. Moreover, the

IC-Index actually reduces the amount of leeway accounting methods normally leave companies, because it makes a bigger part of the company visible. In this sense, intellectual capital theory can actually help analysts shed light on the parts of the company that are presently very difficult to view from the outside.

The most important characteristic of the IC-Index is that it is a self-correcting index. In fact, if the performance of the IC-Index does not reflect the changes of the market value of the company, then either the choice of the indicators, or the choice of weights or the choice of capital forms is flawed. This consideration comes from the fact that the influence of intellectual capital on the value of the company is an accepted truth. Thus, if the IC-Index does not capture this relationship, then obviously the index is measuring the wrong thing (wrong choice of IC categories and IC flows to include), or the right thing wrongly (wrong indicators), or giving the wrong importance to the different factors (wrong weights). The error in itself provides an insight into the level of understanding the company has of itself, the business in which it operates and the strategy it is pursuing. Of course, the progress of IC-Index and market value will not be perfectly similar: some differences can be explained through error variables, imperfections of the markets and external events. When these discrepancies become rather big and frequent, however, it is time for the company to re-examine its IC-Index and maybe to improve it.

The IC-Index™ Approach

London-based Intellectual Capital Services is the pioneer in the development and application of consolidated measures for IC in companies. In fact, this chapter is written around their IC-Index™ approach. This approach was used by Skandia in their 1997 IC Supplement to the Annual Report. For more information, contact Intellectual Capital Services, Ltd, 46 Gray's Inn Road, WC1X 8LR London; http://www.intcap.com; e-mail: intcap@intcap.com.

IC-Index™ is a trademark of Intellectual Capital Services, Ltd., London.

Appendix: A Matter of Scales

As a conclusion to this chapter, we would like to spend a few pages talking about a very interesting property of the intellectual capital theory we have discussed so far. Our focus has been a single company, for obvious reasons. Our background, the origin of the concept of intellectual capital, and a certain appropriateness all point to the direction of studying intellectual capital in the company context. There is nothing, however, to stop us from applying the same concept across different scales.

We have already seen that Skandia has started scaling down its Navigator to the individual level. This allows the employees to track their progress and evolution: the data resulting from this are, of course, very interesting to the company, too. The possibility of seeing a change in an indicator at the end of the year is a source of great satisfaction for the employees, and a sign that the company is moving in the right direction.

Intellectual capital, however, has also been scaled up. The afore-mentioned Intellectual Capital Services has applied the concept on a business network level, while the Market Academy of Stockholm University has published a study applying the Skandia Navigator on a national level, to the Swedish economy.

IC in Networks: the Experience of SND

Let's start with the application on a network level. The Norwegian Industrial and Regional Development Fund (SND) specialises in, among other things, funding small- and medium-sized limited companies (typically between 5 and 250 employees) which form small networks to compete internationally. Typically initiated by one or two companies, these networks could include between three and seven small- or medium-sized companies. Each company would bring to the consortium a unique business activity, resulting in a higher, network-level business system competing with larger companies. Since 1991, this venture capitalist operation has funded the formation of some 600 networks, involving almost 2500 small- or medium-sized companies.[1] Figure 4.3 depicts a typical network.

SND was interested in identifying a measurement that would indicate the non-financial effects of its investments. It decided to develop a specialised IC-index that would measure the growth of intellectual capital both on the individual company level and on the network level. After some research, some ways of creating value were found to have a substantially larger impact on the network-specific growth/decline of IC than others. These forms were:

- value creation by employees
- value creation through relationships
- value creation through business processes
- value creation through innovation or 'productification'.

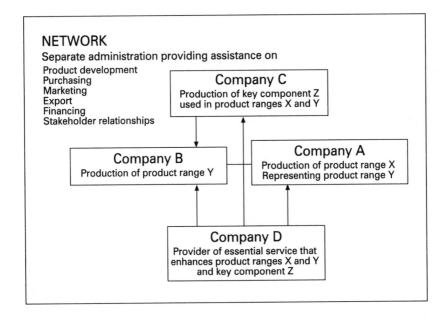

Figure 4.3   A typical network

Given this, strategy-independent indicators were identified for these forms of value creation. The indicators were selected only after extensive research so that they fulfilled the requirements of robustness, precision, and 'dimensionlessness' that we outlined earlier. Using these indicators, indices for each of the ways of creating value were constructed. An aggregated index was also derived.

These indices could then be consolidated by network or by total number of companies assisted. The outcome for some networks are shown in Figure 4.4. An example of the outcome of the process, up to and excluding consolidation is illustrated for one company in Figure 4.5.

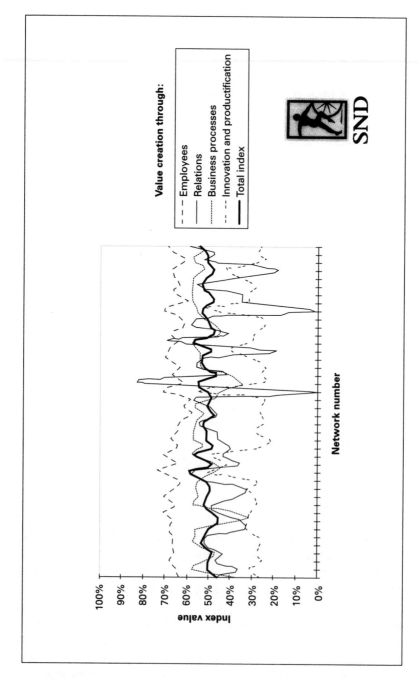

Figure 4.4 Value creation in networks

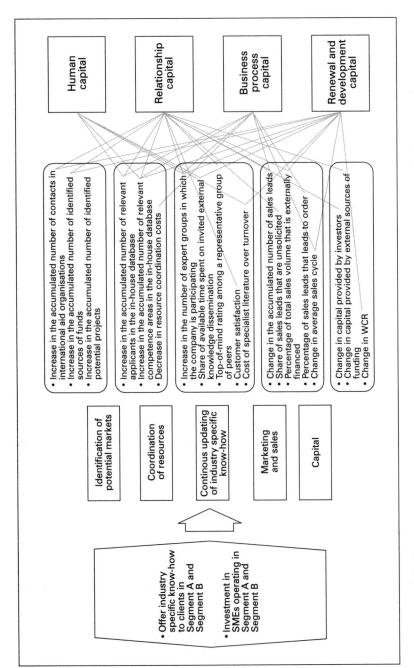

Figure 4.5 Example of IC system/process model of a company in a SND network

IC in Networks: the Experience of AusIndustry

The Business Network Program of AusIndustry, the Australian
Government organisation charged to support businesses, has carried out a
similar study, trying to analyse the intellectual capital it creates in a
network. The point of view in this case, however, was that of the
programme administrator (AusIndustry), rather than that of the network.
In a way, this attempt complements SND's efforts, offering the opposite
point of view.

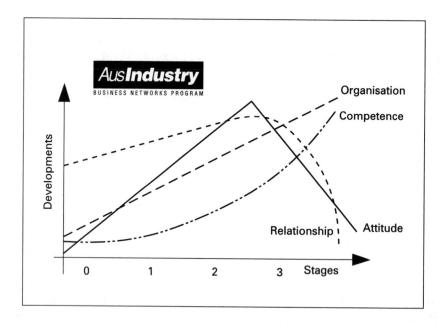

Figure 4.6   Development of different forms of capital

   Networks, in the Australian programme, are usually more separated
from the 'normal' operations of the company, and are used as a means of
expanding into new markets or creating new products. Usually they
belong to one of two categories which we can call networks of scale and
networks of scope. Networks of scale try to gain for its members advantages of scale, performing activities like purchasing, marketing or sales
for all the member companies. Networks of scope aim at the exploitation
of new opportunities, through a combination of the specific competencies
that the members might possess. Obviously, no network falls neatly into
one or the other category, most of them having characteristics of the two.

The results of the study were quite interesting. As the networks went through the different stages of development the programme prescribed, they seemed to be developing different forms of capital. Competencies, for example, were continuously increased (where competencies, in this case, indicated the management ability of the members). From the perspective of AusIndustry, relationship and commitment developed up to the point when the network agreement was formalised, or a new company was created as a joint venture. After that, the network was technically not in the programme anymore; its members were not creating anything new, but were instead running what they had created before. Thus, relationship and commitment decreased gradually. Organisation value remained low for the duration of the product, only to shoot up dramatically when the agreement was formalised. Finally, renewal and development seemed to be independent of programme development. These dynamics are presented in Figure 4.6.

The different indicators were, in this case, grouped both by capital form and by key success factor, to give AusIndustry additional feedback on how it was performing in each of the six areas examined (Figure 4.7). This data allowed AusIndustry to understand, with a clear mind, the areas which could be improved in the future, and those which did not need any improvement.

IC on a Country Level: the Swedish Experience

An attempt to apply the Skandia Navigator on a national level has been made by the Market Academy of the University of Stockholm.[2] Researchers have identified appropriate national indicators for each of the five focus areas. They thus tried to complement the traditional picture of the future prospects of the country, created with financial data, with the more uncommon one drawn through intellectual capital tools. The only slight modification they made to the Navigator was the substitution of the customer focus with a more general market focus. As indicators they used the balance of trade, the honesty standard (obtained through a survey) and the number of overnight stays by foreign tourists for the market focus; the level of education, the average life expectancy and the crime rate for the human focus; the number of personal computers and a business leadership index for the process focus; and finally the expenses in R&D, the number of patents, and the number of business start-ups for the renewal and development focus.

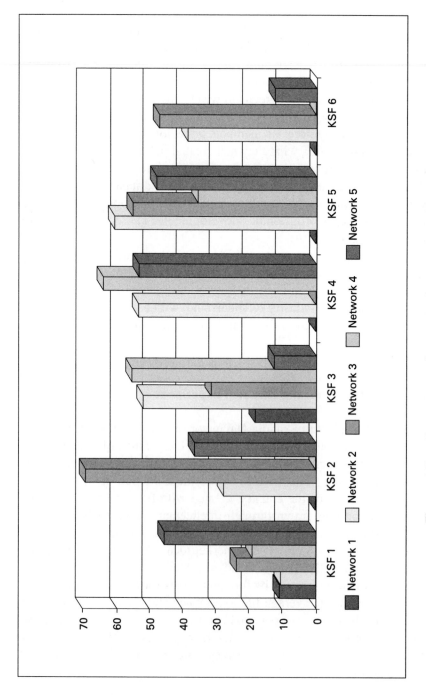

Figure 4.7 Key success factors indices for AusIndustry

What the researchers of the University of Stockholm are aiming to demonstrate is that the value of a country, like the value of a company, is made up of much more than just its economic statistics. Again, this is nothing new; factors such as citizens per hospital bed, pollution, unemployment rates, levels of education, relations with foreign countries, and so on, have always been recognised as important by governments all over the world. All the same, there has never been an attempt to visualise the financial and non-financial aspects of a country at the same time. This simultaneous consideration might encourage governments to see the trade-offs, and thus to have a more complete picture of the status of the country itself.

Naturally enough, not all the theory on IC can be applied to countries. With few exceptions countries do not have strategies, but instead have to balance their duties. More importantly, they are not trying to make money, even though they are (or should) be trying to put their funds to the best use. All the same, we believe that IC considerations on a national level could still yield some interesting political insights. Before that can happen, though, considerable research has to be done.

5 Connecting IC to Shareholder Value[1]

Let's go back to Yankee Finance, the US-based financial company we introduced in last chapter. Their IC experience started from a simple management task, namely to monitor and predict shareholder value. This is nothing special or new. Many companies around the world have this same task as the guiding force behind management action. Indeed, the management of shareholder value as the ultimate goal of a company is now a deeply rooted concept, both in the theory and the practice of management. So, what does this purpose have to do with IC?

Plenty. The creation of shareholder value requires management to be completely conversant with the sources of this value, and with the connection between these sources and the value itself. We can assume that shareholder value is accurately represented by market value.[2] If this is true, then the whole issue is to understand how the market rewards companies for an increase in the sources of value. If we examine again Tables 1.1 and 1.2, it is obvious that in no case, or almost no case, does the value of a company come exclusively from its financial capital. Quite the contrary in fact: the fastest growing companies show an amazing dependance on something else for their value. The fact that these companies are also the highest valued should not surprise us once we identify this 'other' source of value as knowledge and information. As Chapter 1 discussed, knowledge and information follow increasing return curves, which make them all the more attractive, not to mention almost limitless, as sources of value.

Some companies have already realised this, and have started to shift their production approach so that it contains a higher grade of knowledge. American steel mills are the perfect example. In the 1980s they seemed bogged down in the crisis that was affecting heavy industries all over the world. Some of them (Nucor, for example) decided that the only way out was to aim for a smaller scale, more customised production, which would make every ton of steel respond to the specific characteristics set by the clients. The era of the mini-mills was born, and nowadays many of the mills are quite profitable, even though they are operating on a much smaller scale than before. The difference, as they themselves point out, is in the amount of knowledge that each ton of steel contains.

The last chapter introduced the concept of an IC-Index, which is a number that represents the 'bottom line' of intellectual capital management. It also made the point that though the absolute value of the IC-Index is often meaningless,[3] changes in the value do provide the company with valuable information. This chapter will try to connect the changes in IC with changes in shareholder value, and establish a link between the two. To achieve this goal, the sources of market value will be examined first, as well as the evaluation methods for each of them. We will then move on to an analysis of the connection between these sources of value, and especially the ones linked to IC and market value. Throughout the chapter the cases of two companies that have studied the connection betwen their IC and their value will be presented and analysed to exemplify the prescribed actions. We will end the chapter with some considerations on the return on intellectual capital.

Identifying the Sources of Value

In a recent article[4] in the *Harvard Business Review*, Timothy Luehrman of the Sloan School of Management, MIT, observed that the value of companies derives from three main sources:

- operations
- oppportunities
- ownership claims.

These divisions make perfect sense and will thus be used as a starting point of our discussions. Operations indicate all the assets-in-place, that is all the assets which contribute to the normal, day-to-day routine of a company. Opportunities group together the 'possible future operations' of a company, that is all the possible future expansions the company may undertake. Finally, ownership claims represent any shareholding in other companies.

The ownership claims are, for all purposes, part ownerships of another company's operations and opportunities. Therefore, though they do pose separate valuation problems, from an intellectual capital point of view they are neutral if we take the perspective of the mother company. Of course, the mother company can use its management ability to influence decisions in the other companies, but this is a borderline case and it does not change the fact that the value of the ownership claims changes only if the value of the underlying company changes, or if financial capital is invested to increase the stake in the company. Both alternatives do not involve intellectual capital, so we will ignore this source of value in the future discussion.

The impact of intellectual capital is stronger in opportunities than it is in operations. Value from operations can change due to changes in management skills (competence capital) or in process efficiency (structural capital). Almost all changes in intellectual capital, though, have a reflection in changes in value coming from opportunities. Better managers can identify better future directions for the company expansion; better processes can create the opportunity for additional production or involvement in different products; increased training of the workforce can allow for better or more complicated products, which previously were out of reach of the company's possibilities. Like operations above, opportunities are then affected by the management ability to achieve efficiency, too. In other words, the value that the market is willing to credit for those opportunities depends on the management's ability to use them to the full.

Yankee Finance

Let's turn our attention once more to Yankee Finance. The company, as Chapter 4 mentions, operates in the financial product markets and is based in the US. It can be considered medium sized and is regarded in the industry as a new force to be reckoned with and a pathfinder in the generation of new ways of doing business.

During a routine evaluation of their operations, top managers clearly articulated their task as 'monitoring and predicting shareholder value'. Though they had been using intellectual capital measures, they realised that they still did not understand how their (positive) results in IC management reflected on their market value. They had also had a few difficult years financially, and thus they decided that this was the perfect moment to move further down the road of intellectual capital, and try to understand where their market value really came from.

Their first step was to analyse the company's current situation so that they could understand how much of its value came from operations and how much from opportunities. To do that, managers compared the historical series of intellectual capital and financial results with the variations in market value. The results? Apparently, the market was rewarding their operations much more than their opportunities. The company was considered to be a fast converter of the opportunities: as soon as one was spotted on the horizon it was turned into a product. This, of course, was positive, because time-to-market was minimal and there were often benefits to being a first-mover. At the same time there were also negative consequences: opportunities were sometimes converted too early, and so their full value was not exploited.

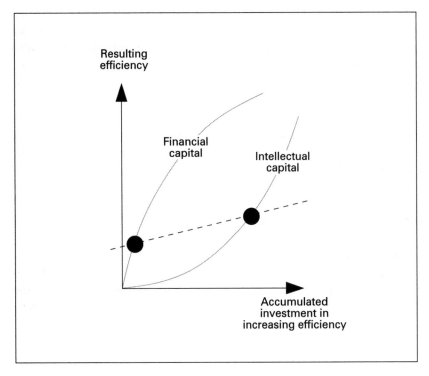

Figure 5.1 Yankee Finance's efficiency in using resources

Managers also examined their effectiveness at using both financial and intellectual capital. Again, this analysis was made through an assessment of past results, plus some benchmarking against competitors and against what managers themselves would qualify as the maximum result possible. Their conclusions were that the company was relatively good at using its intellectual capital but quite bad at exploiting its financial capital (Figure

5.1). The figure itself will be explained later but, for now, suffice it to say that it shows the efficiency in using the company's resources, relative to the accumulated investment in attempting to increase this efficiency.

All this work enabled managers to understand more fully the company's situation, and thus plan a course of action. As we already noted before talking about the IC-Index, giving managers some tools or visual representation which will then spark off discussion is already a remarkable achievement. Whereas before people 'just knew' what the company situation was, now they could see it clearly and discuss it. In a way, this is the transformation of internal, tacit knowledge into external, explicit knowledge.[5]

Yankee Finance managers thus decided that they did not like the situation as it was. They wanted the market to credit their company with more value from opportunities, value they believed they deserved. They also wanted to improve the efficiency with which they used both financial and intellectual capital resources. They thus started a two-pronged programme aimed at monitoring the correlation between market value, financial capital and intellectual capital (which they decided were good proxies for operations and opportunities, respectively), and also at improving the exploitation of opportunities, the market perception of them, and finally the company's efficiency in the use of resources.

Capturing Strategic Insights

The Yankee Finance example shows that the first benefit a company can reap from attempting to link IC to market value is insights into its own nature. Some might say that this is irrelevant, or only a side effect. Quite the contrary. The whole theory on intellectual capital is about rethinking the company and its value roots, as we have pointed out time and again in the book.

Unlike in the process model (see Chapter 3), these reflections are usually new. Where companies normally have a mission statement or a long-term strategy, and have thought their key success factors through, it is extremely rare for managers to sit down and try to understand where the company value comes from. Certainly they will have a rough idea that it comes from the activities and the intangible side, but they will rarely be able to be more precise than that.

Thus, in this first step, it is essential that companies clearly understand what their sources of shareholder value are, as well as their relative importance. This, however, is not enough. Companies need also to understand how well they are turning their operations and their opportunities into value, that is their efficiency in using financial and intellectual capital.

Here, unfortunately, is where problems start. As we know from Chapter 1, financial and intellectual capital in fact follow two fundamentally different economic laws. Whereas financial capital is characterised by diminishing returns, intellectual capital, on the other hand, enjoys increasing returns. A doubling of the investment in efficiency cannot, therefore, cause a doubling of the efficiency rate. If we are considering intellectual capital, the final efficiency rate will be more than twice as high as the initial; if instead the focus is on financial capital, then the final rate will be less than twice as high as the initial one. The graph to convert investment to efficiency will look something like Figure 5.2.

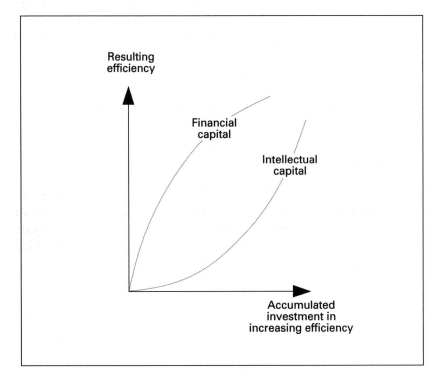

Figure 5.2   Increasing/decreasing returns

As a rule of thumb, a company should be good in whatever most of its value comes from. This is not always true, however. In the case of

Yankee Finance, the company's value came mostly from operations (that is, from financial capital), even though the company itself was much better at managing its intellectual capital. What is important is that managers must make a conscious decision, regarding what the company is supposed to be good at. Obviously, the best situation is to be good at managing both IC and financial capital. This does not happen too often, though, and the resources required to reach a very good efficiency level in using financial capital are often higher than the actual return. Every company should strike its own balance, but the important point is that this balance must be reached through a conscious managerial decision, and not left to natural events.

Machine plc

Let's examine another case. Machine plc is a big European heavy industrial equipment manufacturer. It is regarded as a top performer in the industry, but that industry is a rather predictable and conservative one, and the company has grown to be the same. A couple of years ago, a change in ownership occurred. The new owner sent a very clear message to managers: increase shareholder value rapidly, or be prepared to pay the consequences.

The analysis of the company's value revealed, rather predictably, that the bulk of the value came from the operations rather than opportunities. Moreover, the company was quite good at using its financial capital, whereas its use of intellectual capital was rather poor (Figure 5.3). This, of course, put managers in a very awkward position, because any sizeable increase in the efficiency of use of either financial or intellectual capital would require considerable investment.

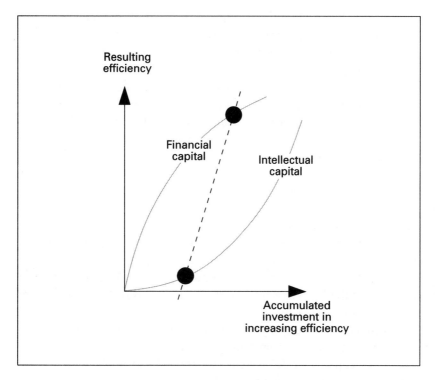

Figure 5.3 Machine plc

The consideration of the graph above shed some additional light on the four strategic alternatives managers had already chosen. In particular, the company could:

■ Buy more equipment: this option implied the conversion of monetary to physical capital. There is no certainty that the strategy would be successful, and indeed, given a stable market situation, expanding the plant to increase output would be counterproductive. If the aim was to increase efficiency, then the already high efficiency would make this strategy at best difficult, at worst damaging to value.
■ Increase the return on assets, that is increase the efficiency. As we remarked above, an increase in efficiency is extremely difficult (and risky) to attain, given the already high level of efficiency.
■ Develop new products. In our terms, this means transforming human capital (knowledge about the products) into structural capital, hoping that this creates a flow to financial capital. Given the situation, counting on intellectual capital seems the only way out, albeit a

costly one. The problem is that the company does not have the human capital necessary to create these new products, nor the ability to turn the human capital into the products, nor the ability to do so efficiently.

▪ Develop new business. A similar strategy to the one above, this entails the creation of new structural capital through the expenditure of financial capital (market research, pilot studies, and so on), in the hope of the generation of a (higher) flow from structural capital to intellectual capital.

The final decision was to implement a combination of the last two strategies, adapted to take the company's particular situation into account. The company started an acquisition spree, 'shopping around' for companies that could generate new product or new business for Machine plc. These companies were set in a newly created division, whose managerial aim was to ensure that maximum revenue was generated from this new knowledge: in the language we introduced above, this translates the goal of the division in increasing IC use efficiency.

To monitor the company's progress in these two areas (creating new IC through acquisition, and improving efficiency in converting this new IC into financial capital), an IC system was created and implemented, monitoring both stocks and flows of capital. In particular, the focus was on the packaging ability (part of intellectual agility), as well as on the new knowledge, on the human capital side. For structural capital, the attention was on the new products, services and relationships developed. Flow indicators also monitored the transformation of one form of capital into another, and the final creation of financial flows were tracked.

The Final Step: Aggregating Indices

Once the sources of value of a company are clear, it is possible to go one step further and try to establish specific relations. Basically, while the purpose previously was to understand how much the market appreciates operations and opportunities, at this stage companies usually try to understand how an increase in any of the stocks of IC or financial capital are appreciated. This, of course, is essential in understanding trade-off relationships between the present (operations) and the future (opportunities). Without this kind of information, managers will not be able to appreciate the impact a given strategy will have on their company's value.

Managers of Machine, for example, aggregated their indicators in four indices: human capital stock, structural capital stock, human to structural capital flow and structural to financial capital flow. These four indices allowed them the control of the key strategic measures and made it possible to correct deviations from the desired values. Their concentration was obviously on the creation of future opportunities: the company had no problem with the current operations, being a market leader and enjoying a remarkable level of efficiency in its plants.

Eighteen months later, Machine's market value had increased by 23 per cent. Moreover, the underlying structure of the company had changed: the percentage contribution of opportunities to value had increased, and managers expected this trend to continue as the new 'innovative' division bore fruit. Also, managers realised that their high efficiency in the use of financial capital, as well as the high absolute amount of physical and financial assets, could be used as a tremendous leverage. Their efficiency in the use of intellectual capital had also increased (Figure 5.4): the relative autonomy that was granted to the new division enabled it to 'start from scratch', and develop new processes which could maximise the use of its intellectual capital resources.

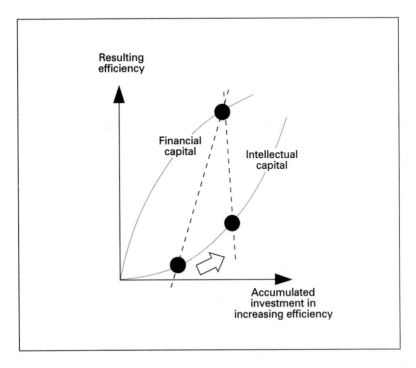

Figure 5.4   Machine plc (after the IC system had been in place)

All of these results, managers said, were a direct consequence of their ability to track closely the development and progress of the strategy. This control, as we mentioned before, was achieved through the creation of an intellectual capital system, and the aggregation of those measures in a few indices, summarising the company situation. These indices allowed managers to control (and in this case increase) market value to a much greater extent than they could ever have done before.

The Bottom Line

This is where all the work the company has done in the creation of an IC system finally pays off. Understanding the importance of IC in the market value of a company is important, but it is only when managers start to understand how the market appreciates changes in the stocks of IC that the real managing can start.

Now, it is possible to quantify the effects of a given investment in IC, through the analysis of the reduction in financial capital and the increase in IC itself. Companies can also consider what impact the different components of intellectual capital have on the market value. This analysis can bring some insights on the importance, or the importance perceived by the market, of each of these components. The value of such an analysis becomes apparent when managers can compare this relevance to the weights they have selected. If the two series of data are different, then there are two possible scenarios.

On one hand, the market might perceive the importance of the components wrongly. In this case, the company should strive to communicate its 'value scale', so that the market can appreciate the company and its actions correctly. If this does not happen, then the market value will be a distortion of the true company value: as managers invest in the truly driving value-enhancing factors of operations or opportunities, the market will not appreciate their efforts correctly. It is important to note that usually this situation is temporary at best. When financial results are announced the market should be able to understand its mistakes, and correctly evaluate the company.

There is, however, a second scenario which might explain a difference between weights and market perceptions: the company can be wrong. If internal discussion (or, once again, financial results) reveal that this is the case, then all the company needs to do is correct those weights, and then re-evaluate its intellectual capital. In this case, we can say once again that the IC-Index is self-correcting. Unlike the considerations we made earlier (see Chapter 4), this time we can clearly pinpoint the problem in the weights: the self-diagnostics of the IC-Index here is much clearer.

Yankee Finance

Yankee Finance developed an IC-Index (which was examined in Chapter 4), as well as a financial capital index and a market value index. These last two were developed using the same methodology described above for the IC-Index, to allow for correct comparisons (Figure 5.5). More information on the creation of these two indices can be found below.

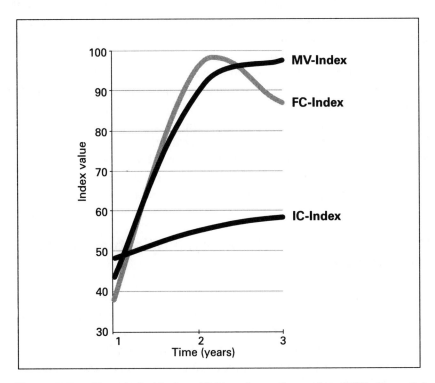

Figure 5.5   Trends in Yankee Finance's market value (MV), financial capital (FC) and intellectual capital (IC)

From the graph, it became clear that initially the market had followed only the company's financial capital, and was therefore giving the company credit only for the value deriving from the operations. The situation had changed, though. It seemed that the leading indicator for market value was now the IC-Index, and no longer the FC-Index. This was probably a result of the company's effort to visualise it through special reports. In fact, even though the company had posted negative financial results for the last year, market value had never fallen, precisely because of the increasing effect IC (and thus opportunities) were having.

Thus, managers needed simply to concentrate on the improvement of efficiency, and the longer-term horizon for their opportunities. Now, two years later, they have achieved good results: their opportunities are appreciated more by the market analysts, and they are no longer perceived as a quick converter, even though their time-to-market is still among the lowest in the industry. As a consequence, their market value has increased by 100 per cent. According to top managers of the company, it was all possible because the whole company had a clear picture of the situation and the goal. This clear picture could not have been delivered to everybody in the company without the help of the graphs and figures reproduced above.

Unlike Yankee Finance, Machine was relatively uninterested in the formal correlation between IC and market value. The management of the company had a crisis on its hands that had to be solved, and solved fast. Thus, they needed to understand the connection and use it, fast, to increase the market value of the company itself. Therefore, they did not formalise this correlation through the construction of additional indices but concentrated their efforts on the creation of intellectual capital, and the market rewarded it with a considerable value increase.

Building Alternative Return on Intellectual Capital Measurements

What we have seen up to now are, for all purposes, two ways of understanding the effect that investment in intellectual capital has on market value, in other words, two forms of return on intellectual capital (ROIC).[6] There are, however, some other ways of getting similar measurements, and this section will give some additional information on the matter.

Generally speaking, there are four ways of looking at the return on intellectual capital and they can be compiled in a matrix. The main problem to solve is to express financial capital and intellectual capital in the same unit of measurement, to allow comparisons. This means that we either have to express intellectual capital in monetary terms, or that we need to construct a financial capital index similar to the IC-Index we explored in Chapter 4. Looking at ROIC from another perspective, it can be estimated by looking at the change in the stocks of both intellectual capital and financial capital, or, indirectly, by looking at the changes in market value. If we chart the two dimensions together, the result is a matrix identifying four different perspectives on return on intellectual capital (Figure 5.6).

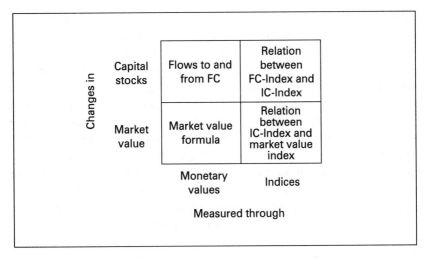

Figure 5.6   Perspectives on return on IC

The choice among the four will depend on the particular attitude and nature of the company, as well as on the type of data available and the specific purpose of the exercise. The advantage of looking at the same problem from four different perspectives, of course, is that the insight gained from each single point of view can be compounded and united into a bigger and far more complete picture.

Let's start with the top left corner. This perspective follows the textbook definition of return on any investment and applies it to intellectual capital. Theoretically, the definition of ROIC is quite simple: it is the ratio between the flows from intellectual capital to financial capital and the flows between financial capital to intellectual capital:

$$\text{ROIC}_1 = \frac{\text{Flows from IC to FC}}{\text{Flows from FC to IC}}$$

However, this ROIC (let's call it $ROIC_1$) does not consider temporal delays at all. An increase in IC capital at a given time might be the result of an investment of a long time before; this is actually not different from more traditional financial investment. The difference, though, is that with intellectual capital it is difficult to understand when the flows originating from one given investment end. 'Sleeper' flows might manifest a long time after the initial investment has taken place.[7] If we assume that it would be possible to wait for all the flows to manifest, then we can construct the $ROIC_1$ perfectly. The flows on the nominator and denominator should of course be discounted to take into account the time variable, but that is certainly not a great hurdle. Thus, while this is probably the most theoretically valid method of measuring ROIC, it is not feasible.

Let's move now towards the bottom left corner of the matrix in Figure 5.6: the measurement of ROIC through the analysis of the change in market value. This is what Machine plc and Yankee Finance have both done. The interesting consideration is that in the analysis of market value changes, the problem of time delays in flows virtually disappears. Financial markets react almost immediately to policy changes, both for strategies affecting intellectual capital and financial capital. Therefore, the increase on intellectual capital becomes relatively easy to see and estimate. Of course, there are still going to be problems when trying to estimate the flows from financial capital to intellectual capital and back: these flows will still be mixed with many others, originating from other intellectual capital or financial investments.

The remaining two alternatives suggest a different way to approach the problem of unit of measurement compatibility. Instead of trying to convert intellectual capital into monetary value, it is possible to convert financial capital and market capital into an index, and then make comparisons between the now compatible indices. In this way a financial index similar to the IC-Index we examined before can be built. Thus, all the different stocks of capital should categorised, weighed and then aggregated into a single index. This way, comparisons between financial and intellectual capital are perfectly possible, and indeed can plot out the relative performance of the company in terms of changes in the two main forms of capital. The analysis will concentrate on stocks, though, only examining flows as the difference between the stocks in two different points in time.

Alternatively, ROIC can be measured by examining the changes in the IC-Index and correlating them with changes in a market value index: this is the bottom right square of the matrix depicted in Figure 5.6. Yankee Finance did exactly this. In this case, what we actually have is a measure of return on the IC-Index. We have already stated that we do not know the relationship between the IC-Index and IC precisely: we know only that they are positively related, and thus an increase in one causes an increase in the other. Therefore, a measurement of return on the intellectual capital index might still yield some interesting results.

It is obvious, then, that a lot more research is needed before we can confidently suggest a measurement for return on intellectual capital. We believe, however, that the four approaches we outlined are the ones that will allow researchers and practitioners to reach this goal.

Towards a New Meaning of Management

Evaluating and managing opportunities and operations require two very different logics. The management of operations is the one we are most accustomed to; operations are normally relatively predictable, if not downright stable. Thus, managers are correct in using traditional planning and strategic management skills when dealing with operations. Similar considerations apply to the evaluation of operations. Because they are stable or predictable, future cash flows coming from them can likewise be forecasted with a good degree of accuracy. The evaluation of operations, therefore, can correctly use traditional discounted cash flow methods.[8]

The problems start when we move from operations towards opportunities. In this case, the traditional rules no longer apply. There is therefore a need to identify new rules more appropriate to the new environment. This need is all the more urgent due to the increased importance that knowledge, which is basically an opportunity, has in the business world, as we outlined in Chapter 1.

The evaluation of opportunities, according to Tim Luehrman, should abandon discounted cash flow methods and use option theory instead. With only a few adjustments, option theory is perfectly capable of giving badly needed insights into the dynamics of opportunities.

The issue then becomes what to make of management. Chapter 1 already examined the changes that the new 'knowledge economy' has brought to the business world in general. What we failed to mention there, though, is that the fundamental shift towards an economy enjoying increasing returns for its most profitable industries is changing also the deeper meaning of management. Traditionally, the managers' task was to plan every detail of the company's actions, in its effort to reach its goal.[9] Traditional management practice assumes a stable environment where the future is going to repeat the past. Under this assumption, observation of the past is presumed to yield some useful insights into future developments. The truth is, it is not happening that way.

Nike did not see Reebok growing into a serious competitor starting from 'a girlie's market', namely aerobics. IBM did not appreciate the challenge Apple's PCs were posing to its products, and later on Apple did not understand the danger of Microsoft and its Windows system. The big consumer-product companies underestimated the own-brand/private label phenomenon until their market share had been significantly cut. Xerox did not see Canon, Ford did not see Honda, Caterpillar did not see Komatsu, Casio and Seiko did not see Swatch.

It seems as though business history is a history of blind men and women, always failing to see where the future lies. And yet we still clutch to the belief that if we plan more, if we spend more time or more money on the planning process, if we develop a better planning tool, we might be able to avoid the pitfalls of blindness. Unfortunately, the chance of this happening are slightly smaller than the chances of finding intelligent life on Mars. The social dynamics of the world are unpredictable.

Traditional management theory is built on two main assumptions:

- that systems strive for equilibrium through negative feedback
- that systems are ruled by linear relationships.

The first assumption implies that social systems, and business organisations among them, live in perpetual states of equilibrium. If anything happens to move the system away from equilibrium, negative feedback loops will initiate corrective actions to bring the situation back into a new, albeit different, state of equilibrium. The second assumption implies that, thanks to linear relationships, the effect of any given action is proportional to the strength of the action itself: large, strong actions will have big effects, while small, weak actions will have limited impact.[10]

Positive feedback economics, however, breaks both of the assumptions. In fact, systems do not tend towards equilibrium because, even when it is only slightly disturbed, positive feedback loops can upset the equilibrium forever. Any movement away from the initial balanced state is thus more likely to escalate into a major crisis than to be absorbed by negative feedback loops.

The new assumption forces us to change our views on environment, company and strategy. Chapter 1 has already reviewed some of the changes at company level. The environment, in this perspective, is not fixed anymore, but an ever-shifting knowledge 'landscape of rubber', where the actions of any company have consequences for all other companies in the same competitive space.[11] Although he did not articulate these assumptions Henry Mintzberg has repeatedly pointed out the fallacies of conventional strategic planning. The first fallacy is to believe that you can predict the future over a certain 'planning horizon', a belief which is the basis for developing a strategic plan. The second fallacy of planning is the inherent detachment of thinkers (strategic planners) from doers (line managers), strategy formulation (the plan) from implementation (subsequent actions), and the intended (the plan) from the emerging (the unexpected). The third fallacy is the fallacy of formalisation, that is an information processing and analysis focus rather than one of internalisation, comprehension and synthesis.[12] Strategic planning, therefore, ultimately loses its significance, because by the time a plan is implemented, the landscape has changed, and the plan is not necessarily meaningful (or optimal) anymore; it could conceivably be quite wrong and threaten the survival of the company.[13] Although conventional planning may be dead, companies obviously set goals and try to 'peep around the corner'. Collins and Porras found that the ability to continuously set 'big hairy audacious' (challenging and often risky) goals was one of the chief characteristics of companies that have prospered for more than half a century.[14]

But if strategy is not planning anymore, what is it? According to Gary Hamel, strategy should become a revolutionary activity.[15] He observes that in today's business world there are three kinds of companies: the rule-makers, the rule-takers and the revolutionaries. The first group includes all the companies that have defined the industries they work in, and are even now reaping the result of their efforts. Coca-Cola, Merrill Lynch, McKinsey, Hertz, IBM and Ford are all part of this first group. The second category encompasses all the companies that have chosen to follow the guidelines set by the leaders: PepsiCo, Avis, Smith & Barney, AT Kearney, Dell and Fiat are good examples of 'followers'. Finally, we find a group of companies who decided to change the rules of the game, and create their own industries. It is this third type of company which is the most successful today, as Virgin Airlines, The Body Shop, Swatch, Norwegian food producer Leiv Vidar, and Nucor Steel have demonstrated. The creation of a new industry might then turn the revolutionary company into the established rule-maker of the industry, until the next revolutionary wave comes around or they can establish some kind of permanent dominion on the business scene. Coca-Cola essentially founded the soft-drinks industry more than a hundred years ago and has managed to survive ever since, notwithstanding all the attacks from competitors.

The question, of course, is how to become strategy revolutionaries. Hamel[15] identifies ten principles. In short, they encourage the company to listen to the dissenting voices, and try to nurture them. A 'yes-culture' is unlikely to produce the next 'Swatch revolution'. The challenge is to identify the hidden conventions the industry is blindly following and challenge the ones that can be challenged, through creative envisioning processes.

The consequence would be a company ready to create opportunities, and not just exploit them, through the harnessing of the creative energies of all employees. However, in this process the end will not be clear at the beginning of the path. Bill Gates probably could not imagine today's situation in the computer industry 20 years ago, when he founded Microsoft. Thus, whereas planning implied a setting of goals and a detailed description of the way these goals were to be reached, strategising requires companies to make their way as they go along. These conclusions are supported by a number of authors who note that the most successful companies interact with the environment and try to shape it as much as adapt to it.[16]

Launched in 1996 the Skandia Future Centres are also a recent excellent example of a concrete attempt simultaneously to forecast and shape trends in the environment. The intention was to help Skandia in 'adapting, hedging, and shaping the future'. It accomplishes this task through inquiring about the future, focusing on what was coming next and what the company could do, not only to become more knowledgeable about it, but also to help shift the business landscape in its favour by actively shaping the future of the industry. This process began with the creation of a 'three generation future team'. The pilot team comprised 25 members chosen from several hundred organisations members across the various operating units and countries of the organisations. The group, which was given some initial discussion topics, communicates regularly using advanced communication technology, and meets occasionally at a specially designed 'energy spot' in Vaxholm, Sweden. One of the main tasks of the future teams will be relationship-building, both within and outside the company.

Skandia Future Centres

Established in 1996, Skandia Future Centres (SFC) represent a *process* which invites a wide variety of organisational members in global project teams to raise the questions that top management should be addressing in the future. Unlike 'corporate retreats', SFCs are places where heterogeneous groups of Skandia employees can meet and discuss what they see as emerging trends. The goal is to identify such trends as soon as possible, in order to ensure that Skandia *adapts* to, and *hedges* itself against, the future. However, it is also a vehicle for Skandia actively to take part in *shaping* the future itself, by seizing the trends at an early stage and redirecting them if necessary. The Centres are nothing more than retreats to which selected employees, with backgrounds as varied as possible, are invited for a short period of time in order to discuss some pre-set topics. The diversity of age, expertise and interest backgrounds of the people involved ensure that the widest possible range of opinions, ideas and perceptions is represented in the dialogues.

If we return to our navigation metaphor, the suggestions above amount to encouraging companies to leave the old, well-known road for the new and uncharted one. If they undertake this course of action, however, companies lose the advantage of clear and familiar maps, and the logic of creating and implementing strategy will have to change as well. In the planning paradigm, well grounded in the assumption of linearity and predictability, the purpose of strategy is to plot a straight line from A (the present state of the company) to B (the desired future state, that is the goals). In the navigation perspective, strategy means indicating quite clearly what is the final goal, and then trying to move in that general direction, but not necessarily in a straight line. As Columbus demonstrated five centuries ago, it might be necessary to go west to reach the East. A single step in the journey will be determined by random external events as much as by the desire to reach the destination. Thus, a step-by-step description of the process is useless: only the ability to create a strong sense of direction remains as a core of the strategy creation process.

Navigation shifts the focus of the company from the short term to the long term. Planning encourages managers to concentrate on a short time horizon, to minimise the effect of unforeseen events: it is common knowledge that plans become worthless when projected more than 12 months forward. Navigation, on the other hand, encourages managers (or leaders, as we said) to take charge and be bold, envisioning the long-term future of the environment and crafting the company's role in it. This envisioning will create only a rough sketch of the future, but that sketch should be enough to motivate the company to strive for the future. In the words of Skandia, 'The future has to become an asset'.[18]

The focus on the future should not take the attention away from the present: to get to the future, the present still needs to be cared for. This brings us to a second very important issue: balancing plans for the future (or advancement activities), which will improve the company's standing and situation, with the activities of the present (or survival activities), which will enable the company to live long enough to get to the future.

The terminology of advancement versus survival is not ours; it comes from Sencorp. Sencorp is one of the few examples of a company that has explicitly addressed this problem. In this company all employees, managers and blue-collar workers alike, have a *responsibility* to manage their own balance between 'survival' and 'advancement' activities.[19] The former simply encompasses all implementation activities for ensuring the survival of the business today. This includes all the work that you want to routinise and the processes you want to re-engineer for increased efficiency. This is when you use hierarchy and more conventional management practices. It is also in the survival mode that operational conversations are played out. The advancement activities run with a different logic. This is when knowledge is developed through non-authoritative, non-intimidating, non-threatening conversations among knowledgeable and equal organisational members. The primary vehicle is a never-ending series of cross-functional and cross-hierarchical projects. The outcome on all levels is new *options* for possible future implementation.

This is easier said than done. An important managerial challenge lies in getting away with the separation of the one from the other. In Sencorp, *every* person is engaged in, and *expected* to engage in knowledge development (advancement), in parallel to the day-to-day business (survival). An additional conceptual, and practical, twist is that the model applies to all activities, even at different levels and scales. While in survival or advancement mode, you still have the same set of three responsibilities, but on a lower scale. For instance, while executing your customer visit – that is, survival, you still have to think about how this could be done differently – that is, advancement 'within' survival.

Sencorp

The family-owned US-based company Sencorp is an example of a company with a management model that balances attention on today with that on tomorrow. Sencorp is the parent of three operating companies – Senco, Senmed, and Senstar – employing some 2000 staff. Senco designs, makes and sells pneumatic fastening systems for a multitude of industries on a worldwide basis. Based on advanced forms of stapling technologies, the company moved into the field of medical wound closure, resulting in the formation of Senmed. Today, Senmed is developing a range of technologies and companies in the medical industry. Senstar is a finance company and primarily operates in the area of industrial leasing. Despite the apparent unrelatedness, in terms of products and markets, among these companies, there is an important consistency in the underlying management logic. During the 1980s, top management in Sencorp tried to come up with a model that could take into account the diverse nature of what they were doing, and thus help them do it better. The Sencorp model defines management responsibilities in terms of three functions (Figure 5.7). A first responsibility is to develop new knowledge in the form of new options that may or may not be implemented later on. A second responsibility is to decide on which options should be implemented, and the third responsibility is to implement options previously chosen. The model is designed to be replicated at any level in the organisation, in fact, these are three management responsibilities of all organisational members. Moreover, activities at different levels fall into the same classification; it is possible, therefore, to have advancement activities in survival activities, for example. The model is applicable at the corporate level, operating company level, at group level and at the individual level.[20]

SOURCE: von Krogh and Roos (1995)

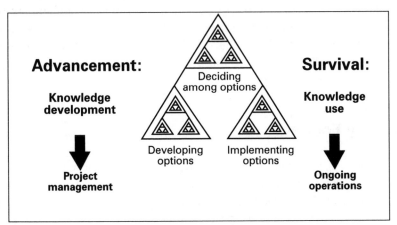

Figure 5.7 The Sencorp management model

Intellectual capital is the result of the advancement activities orientated towards the future, to develop options, and the source of value for the survival activities.[21] Thus, IC is, in many ways, the link between the two kind of activities. Assuming a perspective of managing IC instead of just financial capital to manage the value of a company forces managers always to keep in mind this dual temporal perspective. Where financial results often reward the short-term thinking typical of many companies in years past, IC much more clearly shows the trade-off between present and future.

The bottom line now is the renewal and development of the company, that is the contribution of the project to the future value of the company. Financial capital, and thus the financial contribution, should not be underestimated, but it is only the enabler, the start of the value-creating process for the company. *The real worth of a company is judged through its potential for the future earning capabilities, and this has to become the hallmark against which all projects are measured.*

The drive to improve the (financial) bottom line that swept the business world in the 1980s and in the beginning of the 1990s has crippled many companies. Downsizing and cost-cutting have often eliminated human and structural capital, thus improving the short-term profitability of the company at the expense of the long-term prospects. Sometimes, the disadvantages of this approach have become painfully clear, in a tragi-comic way. At the beginning of 1997, South West Trains, one of the rail franchises operating in Britain, announced they were cancelling many trains. The reason? In an attempt to improve the poor profits of the newly privatised company, they had cut too many personnel, and were now without train operators.

As a consequence of this, the greatest help we can get when embarking on this new version of management and strategy processes comes from having good navigational aids that, at all times, can give us our position, the distance we have travelled, the distance remaining and the speed at which we are travelling.

The Way Forward

The journey is not over; it probably never will be. The exploration of intellectual capital and, more generally, management science is a dynamic process which will always turn up new areas to explore. All the same, the tools we have outlined, and the process of developing these tools can help companies achieve a better understanding of the value-creation process.

From this increased understanding, hopefully, a higher ability to manage the process will develop, with beneficial effects for managers, stakeholders and the society in general. These considerations are true for any company, and the more so the more the company's value comes from intellectual capital as opposed to financial capital – in other words the more the company is ruled by positive feedback rather than negative feedback economics. If the deeper meaning of management has changed, though, then the tools management uses must change as well. Trying to use the old measures in the new world is akin to using the dashboard of a car to operate an airplane. Instead, we need to create a new meaning of management that allows the manager to balance daily implementation with developing options for possible future implementation. Moreover, more than just financial data must be monitored. We have already started the process through the examination of different forms and flows of intellectual capital, the consolidation of these indicators into a few information-rich indices, and the examination of the sources of value creation.

The IC-Index can give managers the pulse of the company's intellectual capital situation. It can warn them of sudden changes, and thus encourage them to look into the causes of these changes, possibly through the lower-level indices. On its own, of course, it is severely limited, because it does not explain the reason for any of the changes. Like all summary measurements, though, it is invaluable in its ability to describe the situation quickly.

It is also clear that the IC-Index is a first step on the road to relate market value to IC. This correlation is extremely important, of course, because the increase in market value (and thus shareholder value) has to be the objective of any manager worthy of the name. Without a way to sum up the IC situation, any correlation to market value (itself an aggregate and summary measure) would be impossible.

Finally, IC can also explain why so many companies today have problems in increasing their value, any good move they make gaining them only a temporary respite, whereas other companies seem never to go wrong. The increasing/decreasing return graph demonstrates that this is only partly due to management skills, but also (and perhaps more) to the particular IC/financial capital balance that the companies present.

What remains to be done? There is still a great need to test and determine more precisely the market value formulation. Better tests of correlation between IC and market value are needed, and more research needs to go into the study of the time delays, so that they can be included in the picture as well. Still, the tools we describe can give managers invaluable new insights, and at a relatively low cost in terms of financial expenditure and effort. For this reason, more and more companies are experimenting with IC. This has started a snowball effect, where leading companies are effectively forcing competitors to adopt an IC approach, so that they can compete effectively.

Notes

Chapter 1

1. The company's end of 1996 total.

2. Number of common shares outstanding multiplied by the price per share as of 14 March, 1997.

3. *Fortune 500* ranking, 28 April, 1997.

4. The use of the replacement value for assets, however, raises the question of the evaluation of irrepleceable, illiquid or unique assets. In most cases, though, these assets are not present in the balance sheet in the first place, so they shoud not be considered in this calculation either.

5. D.V. Fites: "Make your dealers your partners", *Harvard Business Review*, March–April 1996, pp. 84–95.

6. This puts people in the strange situation of being both a decreasing and an increasing return factor, depending on whether they are used as labour or as source of knowledge and information. It is thus up to the company to use its workforce as a real competitive advantage, exploiting its unique knowledge, or as replaceable labour.

7. D. Kline: "The alchemy of wealth", in *Market Forces*, posted on the Internet at: http://www.hotwired.com/market/95/49/index1a.html

8. W. B. Arthur: "Positive feedbacks in the economy", *Scientific American*, February 1990, pp. 80–85; B. Wysocki, Jr: "The wealth of notions", *Wall Street Journal*, 22 January 1994.

9. W. B. Arthur: "Increasing returns and the new word of business", *Harvard Business Review*, July–August 1996, pp. 100–9.

10. When Arthur talks about knowledge-intensive industries, he is really referring to high technology industries. Do positive returns also apply to low-tech, knowledge-intensive companies? Does a law firm enjoy positive or negative feedback? As far as services go, Arthur's answer is that all services are in a hybrid situation, with increasing returns regulating the long term and diminishing returns governing the short term. That is because there are regional limits to the reach of service companies, which means that returns will be diminishing. Franchise chains, as well, we might add, as the development of transports and communication, are reducing the limiting power of diminishing returns, and creating positive feedback loops into the system. Home banking, for example, will most certainly be a positive return area, with many banks fighting to achieve the top spot in the new segment.

It seems, therefore, that the distinguishing feature of increasing return industries is their intense use of knowledge, not their technological content. It would thus be more appropriate to talk about increasing return resources than industries: knowledge presents increasing returns no matter what industry it is used in. Moreover, it is important to notice that increasing returns do not apply to all intangible resources: brands, for example increase with their use but can also be ruined by a failed brand extension, an instance of increased use.

11. It is quite possible that increasing returns are only a phase industries are going through. As industries mature, returns might become once more diminishing. Therefore, returns in this case can be drawn as an S-curve, increasing at first as the resource in question is used more, and then decreasing after a while (Figure 1N.1). Arthur admits that some products pass through an increasing return phase to stabilise later on a diminishing return, but the topic is not developed. More research is definitely needed on the subject.

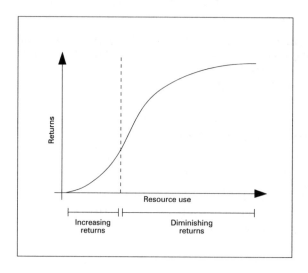

Figure 1N.1   Returns on resources

12. This activity is what Mintzberg and Quinn call pattern recognition, according to them a fundamental ability for managers today; see H. Mintzberg & J. Quinn: *The Strategy Process* (2nd edn), Prentice-Hall, Englewood Cliffs, NJ, 1994.

13. These commando units, by the way, bear more than a passing resemblance to the hunting organisation Hurst speaks of. See D. Hurst: *Crisis & Renewal*, Harvard Business School Press, Boston, MA, 1995.

14. At this stage knowledge, competence and capabilities will be used interchangeably to indicate all the knowledge-based constructs, even though authors have used different names for their concepts before. While the concepts are not exactly the same, their differences, especially for our purposes, are minimal, and thus the concepts themselves can be grouped together.

15. Even though it is a generally accepted distinction, doubts have been cast recently over the tacit–explicit dichotomy. According to the autopoietic epistemology school, knowledge is private and cannot be explicit, only tacit; 'explicit knowledge' is actually data which help other people to create their own knowledge. Pursuing this point, though, would force us into an epistemological debate which is beyond the scope of this book. For argument's sake, we will therefore accept the tacit–explicit distinction, which will enable us to reach interesting insights more easily. See F. J. Varela, E. Thompson & E. Rosch: *The Embodied Mind*, MIT Press, Cambridge, MA, 1992, for the autopoiesis view; and M. Polanyi: *Personal Knowledge*, Routledge, London, 1958, for the tacit–explicit knowledge distinction..

16. This is what has also been called the knowledge-creating spiral: I. Nonaka: "The knowledge-creating company", *Harvard Business Review,* November–December 1991, pp. 96–104.

17. Note that the act of codification is a reflection on the subject in itself, and thus implies a tacit to tacit movement.

18. See for example G. von Krogh & J. Roos: "Conversation management", *European Management Journal*, XIII, (4), 1995, pp. 390–4.

19. G. Hamel & C. K. Prahalad: "Strategic intent", *Harvard Business Review*, May–June 1989, pp. 63–76; W. Ouchi: "Markets, bureaucracies and clans", *Administrative Science Quarterly,* XXV, 1980, pp. 129–41.

20. A. Webber: "What's so new about the new economy?", *Harvard Business Review*, January–February, 1993, pp. 4–12.

21. There also other, more hidden, advantages to supplying core products to competitors. First of all, market dominance positions, while heavily regulated in the finished products stage, are much more tolerated in the core product markets. The market for ultra-flat TV and monitor screens is almost a monopoly, but nobody is even dreaming of intervening. If the same market situation were to develop in the market of laptop computers, one of the downstream products for flat screens, all kinds of anti-monopoly regulations would come in force, and block the company. Moreover, through the offer of a

very competitive core product, the company is discouraging competitors from the internal development of competing or substitute products. This creates a dependency of competitors on the company's supply, which the company itself can exploit if it so chooses. See G. Hamel & C. K. Prahalad: *Competing for the Future*, Harvard Business School Press, Boston, MA, 1994.

22. To be able to achieve this widespread application of skills and knowledge, companies must be able to think holistically, going beyond the limited logic of the strategic business unit and embracing the entire company. In the terms of the learning organisation that we have described above, this skill can be thought of as system thinking at a higher level: the purpose in this case is to understand all the systems the company belongs to, and where the competence in question can find a profitable application. Honda is the typical example of a successful strategy of cross-application of competencies. Honda's competitiveness on engines has been built through its experience as a motorbike manufacturer. The company then moved to cars, using their reliable and powerful engines as a competitive advantage. Knowledge on engines was then compounded through an expansion towards lawnmowers, apparently a totally unrelated market.

23. J. Klein & P. Hiscocks: "Competence development: a practical toolkit" in G. Hamel and A. Heene (eds): *Competence-based Competition*, Wiley & Sons, Chichester, 1994.

24. R. Eccles: "The performance measurement manifesto", *Harvard Business Review*, January–February, 1991, pp. 131–7.

25. At times it felt as if having quality measures was a status symbol.

26. See for example C. Fornell: "A national customer satisfaction barometer: the Swedish experience", *Journal of Marketing*, 1992, pp. 6–21.

27. R, Kaplan & D. Norton: "The Balanced Scorecard – Measures That Drive Performance", *Harvard Business Review*, January–February 1992, pp. 71–9.

28. J. Kurtzman: "Is your company off course? Now you can find out why", *Fortune*, 17 February 1997, pp. 58–60.

29. R. Kaplan & D. Norton: *The Balanced Scorecard,* Harvard Business School Press, Boston, MA, 1997.

30. L. Edvinsson & M. Malone: *Intellectual Capital: Realizing Your Company's True Value by Finding Its Hidden Brainpower*, Harper Business, New York, NY, 1997.

31. For more on Skandia's standard, see next chapter.

32. Quoted in R. Karlgaard: "SEC loves IC", Forbes ASAP, 7 April 1997.

33. For more information, see H. Itami with T. Roehl: *Mobilizing Invisible Assets*, Harvard University Press, Cambridge, MA, 1987.

34. For more information, see G. Hamel & A. Heene (eds): *Competence-based Competition*, Wiley & Sons, Chichester, 1994.

35. For more information, see P. Senge: *The Fifth Discipline*, Doubleday Currency, New York, 1990.

36. We will assume in this book an autopoietic epistemological perspective. Crudely simplified, that means that knowledge is a personal thing, and so an organisation cannot possess it.

Chapter 2

1. Our focus on the achievement of a measurement reflects the considerations we have made before on languaging. If we can manage to express IC through numbers, then we will have created a language everybody can understand and use to compare and discuss specific situations. The trick, of course, is to choose and collect meaningful numbers as opposed to random ones, and to establish a clear meaning for all of them.

2. See Chapter 4 in this book.

3. For more information on financial capital and its management, R. Brealey & S. Myers: *Principles of Corporate Finance*, McGraw-Hill, New York, 1996, or J. F. Weston & T. E. Copeland: *Managerial Finance*, The Dryden Press, Chicago, 1986.

4. J. Tobin: "A general equilibrium approach to monetary theory", *Journal of Money, Credit and Banking*, I, 1969, pp. 15–29.

5. Arbetsgruppen Konrad, K.E. Sveiby (ed.): *Den Osynliga Balansräkningen*, Affärsvärldens Förlag, Stockholm, 1989.

6. We realise the notion of company boundaries is far from certain and accepted, and therefore the definition of external participants is problematic as well. For the sake of brevity, however, we will consider external participants to be all those without a formalised hierarchical dependence on the company's management. We are well aware, though, that continued relations with these external agents can actually make the company boundaries fuzzy enough to consider them internal.

7. For more information, see K. Sveiby: *The New Organizational Wealth*, Berret-Koehler, San Francisco, CA, 1997.

8. H. Saint-Onge: "Tacit knowledge: the key to the strategic alignment of intellectual capital", *Strategy & Leadership*, March–April, 1996, pp. 10–14.

9. N. Bontis: "Managing knowledge by diagnosing organizational learning flows and intellectual capital stocks", presentation to the *Creating Value through Knowledge Management* conference, San Francisco, 20 February, 1997.

10. For more information see A. Brooking: *Intellectual Capital*, Thomson Business Press, London, 1996.

11. S. Albert & K. Bradley: *The Management of Intellectual Capital*, Working paper, LSE – The Business Performance Group, February, 1995.

12. This is exactly what all the literature on core competencies has been concentrating on, even though the 'core' bit limits their focus further. For more information on core competence see Chapter 1 and G. Hamel & C. K. Prahalad: *Competing for the Future*, Harvard Business School Press, Boston, MA, 1994.

13. Assuming you can speak of hard and soft parts of intellectual capital, a soft concept in itself.

14. J. Roos & G. von Krogh: "Figuring out your competence configuration", *European Management Journal*, X (4), 1992, pp. 422–7.

15. Even though we use the term knowledge, our meaning does not share all the characteristics of knowledge as they have been evidenced in centuries of studies. For example, knowledge capital cannot be embedded or encoded (embedded knowledge capital is structural capital), and can only be explicit and never tacit. We are not trying to say that there is no such thing as tacit or embedded knowledge. We just prefer to give these two concepts different names from knowledge.

16. Skills can be tacit or explicit, this separates them from knowledge, which, *as a component of competence*, can only be explicit. Many natural talents imply skills which cannot be communicated in words: singing, playing an instrument, baking, or oratory are all skills with at least a tacit component in them. Tacit skills cannot be transmitted through explicit teaching, only through observation or through practical experimentation. Explicit skills, on the other hand, are easier to communicate because they can be codified into words and (at least partially) shared across the organisation.

17. A recent ad for their financial services division claims: "Our PEP [Personal Equity Plan] is up, up and away (unlike me)" over a photo of Branson, referring to his failed attempt to circumnavigate the world in a hot-air balloon.

18. G. D. Smith, D. R. Arnold & B. G. Bizzel: *Business Strategy and Policy*, Houghton Muffin, Boston, MA, 1991.

19. G. Hamel & C. K. Prahalad: "Strategic intent", *Harvard Business Review*, May–June 1989, pp. 63–76.

20. For more on the company's culture, see the sub-section on Organisational Capital later in the chapter.

21. Therefore, intellectual capital agility is the normative side of knowledge, which Hamel and Prahalad, in their first definition of core competence, included in the concept. See C. K. Prahalad & G. Hamel: "The core competence of the corporation", *Harvard Business Review*, May–June 1990, pp. 79–91. Other authors have referred to the same thing as meta-competencies, see J. A. Klein & P. G. Hiscocks: "Competence-based competition: a practical toolkit", in G. Hamel & A. Heene (eds): *Competence-based Competition*, Wiley & Sons, Chichester, 1994.

22. See R. Stacey: *Strategic Management and Organisational Dynamics*, Pitman, London, 1993.

23. We use enactment in the sense Karl Weick of the University of Michigan did: understanding and shaping the environment thourgh the company's actions. See K. Weick, *op. cit.* (note 16 in Chapter 5).

24. This is not true when it comes to highly personalised services such as consulting: in this case, it is quite common that when account managers or consultants leave the company they take some of the clients with them. These relations should probably be categorised under Social Behaviour Capital, examined earlier in the sub-section on Attitude Capital.

25. In terms of transaction theory, a market structure has to be replaced by a hybrid with some market and some hierarchical characteristics. See O. Williamson: *Markets and Hierarchies: Analysis and Anti-trust Implications*, The Free Press, New York, NY, 1975.

26. T. E. Vollmann, C. Cordon & H. Raabe: "Supply chain management: making the virtual organization work", M2000 Executive Report, 19 February, 1996.

27. P. Kotler: *Marketing Management* (6th ed.), Prentice-Hall, Englewoods Cliffs, NJ, 1988.

28. C. Fornell: "A national customer satisfaction barometer: the Swedish experience", *Journal of Marketing*, LVI, January, 1992, pp. 6–21.

29. L. Edvinsson & M. Malone: *Intellectual Capital*, Harper Business, New York, 1997.

30. It is important to remember, though, that such a trade would follow the law of increasing returns, being based on knowledge assets. See the section 'New Economic Laws for the New World' in Chapter 1.

31. We will examine some of these efforts later; most of the intranets networks, however, function along these lines and with these aims.

32. G. Hofstede: *Cultures and Organisations*, HarperCollins, New York, NY, 1991.

33. R. Nelson & S. Winters: *An Evolutionary Theory of Economic Change*, Harvard University Press, Cambridge, MA, 1982.

34. G. Petrash: "Dow's journey to a knowledge value management culture", *European Management Journal*, XIV, 1996, pp. 365–73.

35. This activity is usually called knowledge management, even though we believe the term to be misleading (how do you manage knowledge if it is a personal construct?). All the same, as we will see in Chapter 4, these databases can create considerable competitive advantage.

36. Skandia: *Value Creating Processes,* Supplement to Skandia's 1995 Annual Report, 1996.

37. The requisite of interaction for the creation of a culture actually plays against the home-working concepts: if employees do not interact together, then no common culture is created, with all the notorious deleterious effect.

38. For more information see V. Perrone: 'The forms of capital', paper presented at the *16th SMS Conference*, Phoenix, AZ, 10–13 November 1996.

39. There can be a symbolic capital of the relationship, but then the relationship itself warrants separate analysis for organisational capital, because it has turned into an organisational unit of its own.

40. The exceptions being V. Perrone: *op. cit.* (note 38) and N. Bontis: *op. cit.* (note 9).

41. K. Sveiby: *Intellectual Capital and Knowledge Management*, posted on the Internet at:
    http://www2.eis.net.au/~karlerik/KnowledgeManagement.html#KMInitiatives.

42. These measures are essential to choose between alternative strategies to develop IC and the company value in general. Note that the return on intellectual capital does not have to be a monetary value, even though this would make it easier to compare and understand. See G. Roos & J. Roos: "Intellectual performance: exploring an intellectual capital system in small companies", *Long Range Planning*, XXX (3), 1997, pp. 413–26.

43. This of course creates all kinds of problems keeping employees' competencies and skills refreshed enough, so that when the time comes for them to use them they are not too rusty.

Chapter 3

1. This quotation and all the others in this chapter come from interviews with the people involved during the months of March and April 1997.

2. Note that the term manageable list is relative and depends on a judgement by management itself on how many indicators/KSFs they are ready to handle.

3. Always remember that COSA uses the term 'indicators' for what we normally call 'key success factors': we are using our language, instead of the original COSA one, to avoid confusion.

4. For more information on the Navigator, see Chapter 4 and Skandia: *Visualising Intellectual Capital in Skandia*, Supplement to the 1994 Annual Report, 1995.

Chapter 4

1. J. Roos & G. Roos: "Valuing intellectual capital: the next generation", *Financial Times Mastering Management Journal*, May 1997.

2. Though shareholder and market value are not exactly the same, it is possible to say that shareholder value is positively related to market value; thus, an increase in the former will cause an increase in the latter.

3. See Chapter 2: The Flows of Intellectual Capital.

4. This section draws heavily on J. Roos & G. Roos *op. cit.* (note 1).

5. See Chapter 3: Outline the Drivers of Future Earnings.

6. This example is taken from J. Roos & G. Roos *op. cit.* (note 1).

Appendix to Chapter 4

1. It should be noted that this network approach has become a role model for similar initiatives in Australia, Canada and New Zealand.

2. Market Academy Stockholm University: *Welfare and Security*, 1997.

Chapter 5

1. This chapter draws heavily on G. Roos & J. Roos, 'Linking intellectual capital to shareholder value', Working Paper, August 1997, International Institute for Management Development, Lausanne, Switzerland.

2. This, of course, requires a company to be traded in some form or another. Even if the company is privately owned, managers usually have a rough idea of what a company could be worth on the market.

3. There are exceptions: if you assume particular perspectives, and can safely say that at a particlar point in time the Index was zero or close to zero, then obviously the absolute value in itself becomes relevant. This, however, is only due to the fact that in this case the absolute value IS a measure of relative change in the IC-Index, because we know that the Index itself was zero previously.

4. T. Luehrman: "What's it worth? A general manager's guide to valuation", *Harvard Business Review*, May–June 1997, pp. 132–42.

5. I. Nonaka: "The knowledge creating company", *Harvard Business Review*, November–December 1991, pp.96–104. Note that if we accept a self-referential epistemological perspective, there is no explicit knowledge: in this case, generating this kind of report will be akin to transforming knowledge into information, which will then be used (through language and discussion) to generate new knowledge.

6. As we will show later, we are actually interested in the return on the investment in intellectual capital. Thus, it is probably more correct to call it Return on Intellectual Capital Investment (ROIC): it is in fact more similar to the traditional Return on Investments (ROI) than the Return on Assets (ROA). A proper ROIC index would measure the company results given a certain level of the stock in intellectual capital.

7. This issue connects with a bigger problem. With IC it is difficult to isolate the flows originating from the company's actions from the 'background noise', or any other environment variable. If the company undertakes an enormous campaign of communication, and then earns media acclaim for the way it handles, say, sexual harassment allegations against a top manager, then the two effects (communication campaign plus positive 'free' coverage of the sexual harassment crisis) will add up, and most probably in an exponential way. The communication campaign is obviously an attempt to increase the image and brand name of the company (a component of structural capital), and the positive coverage will achieve the same result. So how do you separate the two effects? The answer is, you probably cannot. Due to the increasing return nature of intellectual capital, the communication campaign and the positive media attitude would not have had the same effect if the two had been separated by some time. In a way, a similar phenomenon happens with financial investments as well: tax exemptions can suddenly make an investment much more convenient than it was before. However, in this case the two sources of returns can be clearly separated, and the ROI can be calculated for both alternatives (with or without government subsidy). Moreover, synergy effects for financial investments are smaller and less frequent than those occurring with IC.

8. Even among discounted cash flow methods the choice is vast. Given the elaboration power at the disposal of everybody through the use of spreadsheet software packages, Luehrman suggests the use of the adjusted present value technique. According to this technique, the sources of operational cash flows are identified and then the net present value of cash flow calculated for each of them. These net values are then added up to arrive at a final company value. See T. Luehrman *op. cit.* (note 4).

9. This line of thinking translated into the typical planning model of scan–create alternatives–choose–implement, see for example D. Lynch: *Corporate Strategy*, Pitman Publishing, London, 1997. Even the addition of 'emergent strategies' did not really change the traditional rules of the game. See H. Mintzberg and J. Waters, "Of strategies, deliberate and emergent", *Strategic Management Journal*, July–September 1985.

10. In short, social systems are complex adapting systems, regulated by chaos theory; see R. Stacey: *Strategic Management and Organizational Dynamics* (2nd edn), Pitman, London, 1996.

11. For more on viewing organisations and the environment as complex adaptive systems, see: D. Oliver & J. Roos: "The poised organization: navigating effectively on knowledge landscapes", paper posted on the Internet at: http://www. imd. ch/fac/ roos/paper_po.html

12. H. Mintzberg, "The fall and rise of strategic planning", *Harvard Business Review*, May–June 1994.

13. R. Stacey: *Managing Chaos*, London, Kogan-Page, 1992.

14. J.C. Collins and J.I. Porras, *Built to Last*, Century/Random House, London, 1996.

15. G. Hamel: "Strategy as revolution", *Harvard Business Review*, July–August 1996, pp. 69–82.

16. Among others, see G. Hamel & C. K. Prahalad: "Strategic intent", *Harvard Business Review*, May–June 1989, pp. 63–76; K. Weick: *The Social Psychology of Organizing* (2nd edn), Random House, New York, 1979.

17. For more information on Skandia Future Centres, see D. Oliver & J. Roos: *Skandia Future Centers*, IMD case no GM624, 1996.

18. Skandia: *Power of Innovation*, Supplement to the 1996 Interim Report, 1996.

19. To use the language of Collins and Porras (see note 14), whereas survival would be telling the time, advancement would be to build the clock that last.

20. For a fuller discussion of the Sencorp management model, see Chapter 10 in G. von Krogh and J. Roos, *Organizational Epistemology*, Macmillan, London, 1995.

21. Day-to-day survival activities can enhance IC, for example by suggesting ways to improve process efficiency, or by strengthening the existing relationships. As we mentioned in Chapter 5, however, the model can be applied to activities at different levels; this improvement in IC, then, comes from the advancement part of the survival activities.

Index of Names

3M: 40

A
American Airlines: 45
America On-line: 13
Apple: 11, 13, 40, 45, 118
   Macintosh: 11, 13
Aristotle: 17
Arthur Andersen: 46–7
   AA On-line: 46
Arthur, Brian: 12
AT Kearney: 119
AusIndustry: 98–100

B
Battery: 61, 64–5, 67, 73, 75–6,
   87–8
Baumgartner, Vito: 67
Bell: 45
Bertelsmann: 34
Betamax: 11–12
The Body Shop: 119
Bontis, Nick: 32–3
Branson, Richard: 37
British Airways: 45
British Petroleum: 43
British Telecom: 45
Brooking, Annie: 33–4

C
Canadian Imperial Bank of
   Commerce: 32
Canary Wharf: 9
Canon: 118

Carendi, Jan: 67
Casino: 44
Casio: 118
Caterpillar: 3–4, 38, 59, 67, 73, 77,
   118
   COSA: 59–61, 67, 77
   Mec-Track: 60–1, 63, 68–70,
      73–4, 87
Chevron: 49
The Coca-Cola Company: 2–3, 119
Collins, James: 119
Columbus, Christopher: 121
CP/M: 11

D
Dell: 119
Dow Chemicals: 23, 48

E
Eccles, Robert: 19, 22
Exxon: 2–3

F
Fiat: 119
Fites, Don: 4, 67
Fornell, Claes: 44
Ford: 10, 118–19
Fortis: 21
Fortune: 1

G
Galileo: 18
Galbraith, John Kenneth: 4
Gates, Bill: 120

139

Index of Topics